TO DEBBIE

GOD BLESS & THANKS

Dean

Dreamers, Winners, Heroes and an Angel

by William "Deacon" Balliew

Honey Locust Press
Ranger, Georgia

DREAMERS, WINNERS, HEROES AND AN ANGEL

Honey Locust Press
Copyright ©2008 William "Deacon" Balliew
All Rights Reserved

ISBN 1-60364-003-7
ISBN-13 978-1-60364-003-9

Included stories copyrighted to:
The Calhoun Times
The Chattanooga News-Free Press
Atlanta Magazine
Tony Reynolds
(see attributions page for details)

For information, contact:
info@honeylocustpress.com
or
Honey Locust Press
PO Box 205
Ranger, GA 30734

Table of Contents

Introduction

William W. "Deacon" Balliew's work is well known in Gordon County, and for that matter, throughout much of the world. Deacon has visited foreign countries carrying the message of the Winners Club to organizations interested in The Winners Club concept. He has been the recipient of many awards, at the local, state and national levels. He has been the recognized by three United States Presidents, including an invitation by President Jimmy Carter for his group to visit the White House.

But even though it is impossible to separate Deacon's name from the stories in this book, the book is not about Deacon, and he has been adamant about that. It is about people—children and adults—who have made amazing changes, who met unbelievable challenges and overcame them, because they were loved and accepted, and had the will to succeed.

As you read this book, once in a while you'll no doubt get tears in your eyes. But remember that every story, no matter how sad some of them may seem at times, is a success story. Every one of these kids, most of them now adults, is a winner and a hero. But they all started out as dreamers, just as Deacon did, and with help from others achieved many of those dreams.

Without going too much into numbers and specifics, let's take a look at some of the things that these dreamers accomplished.

In 1968, a Boy Scout troop was formed that became the core of what was to be named The Winners' Club. In 1973, local agencies began to refer families and kids to The Winners' Club for help, because it was recognized as a way to help kids that were having trouble getting help elsewhere.

Kids came and went, some for longer times than others, but between 1973 and 1980, twenty young people were involved in a Club study of those who had been involved in the Winners Club for two or more years.

Six of those twenty young people were mentally challenged.

Two of those six were very athletic. One lettered in football, and another participated in track setting a 200-meters dash in record time and won a gold medal for it.

One of those six was very shy and would hardly talk, but Deacon and his wife Inez found that she had a voice like an angel. Eventually she and other members of The Winners Club sang for President and Mrs. Carter, at their invitation.

Of the remaining fourteen:

- All finished high school
- Ten lettered in various sports
- Two became Eagle Scouts
- One attended and graduated from the police academy.

- Eight entered college and one entered graduate school. All graduated successfully.
- One now has a master's degree
- All fourteen have successful families with children who have broken their previous patterns.

There is more success we could describe here, but we'll let it rest there for those twenty members. It's not all about those twenty, though.

Over the thirty-seven years The Winners' Club was under Deacon's guidance, over six hundred troubled young people passed through the doors of the Club. Some were there for only a short time, some were there for years. No matter what, all felt the unconditional love and acceptance that Deacon and Inez, his late wife, gave by the armload to all of them.

It is Deacon's hope that, as you read these stories, you will gain a better understanding of how able some of those labeled as "disabled" can be, how capable the handicapped can become, and how the challenged are able to rise to the challenge, when given encouragement and love. Please note: the stories themselves are true, but names and some locations have sometimes been changed, to protect the privacy of those involved.

This book is not to make Deacon rich. Deacon has an adopted son, Spunkie, and you will read more about him in this book. The profits from this book all go into a trust fund for Spunkie, to help provide for him and his needs after Deacon is gone. It's a good cause, and one we hope you won't mind supporting by your purchase of this book.

One other thing: when Deacon first approached us about his book, one of the things he insisted upon was that his "voice" should remain genuine in what he wrote. He had considered having someone ghostwrite his book, but after giving that some thought, he decided against it. He wanted his book to sound like him talking to you, the Reader, not like someone's idea about how he should sound.

For that reason, very little editing has been done to the narrative and dialogue, except to catch obvious typographical and spelling errors that creep in when our backs are turned. Except for the articles written by outside authors, what you read here is Deacon talking, and for the most part unchanged.

"Santa don't take presents to Heaven"

Every star in heaven is different. Each one's shape, size, brightness, color and position has a slight variation to it.

Regardless, each one is a star. Every star has a purpose and a name. God's word tells us that He counts the number of stars and gives them all names.

We cannot see them in the light of day, but we know they are there to light up the sky when it is their time to shine.

It is the same with God's creatures here below. Just as the stars in heaven have a course to follow, the same is true of those living on Earth.

The North Star guides ships at sea. The Three Wise Men followed the Star to where the Christ Child was born; so do we here on the earth follow stars.

I have been blessed to know, see, follow, love and be loved by hundreds of God's stars here on earth. I want to tell you about one of the brightest stars I have ever been around, and how this star continues to affect the lives he touches, especially mine.

It is a Christmas story of sorts, I guess. You will probably agree when I say this is a story about a never-ending love that found its expression in a special holiday season.

Scottie "Spunkie" Keener is a young man who came to live with my family 20 years ago. He was only 8. The two of us have been seen together so much now, that he's gotten the nickname "Deacon's Shadow."

I have worked with individuals with personal challenges most all my life. I'm a blessed man, because my time spent with these people has meant as much to me as I believe it has to them.

I have always said that the mentally challenged are God's chosen people, living here and sharing their absolute unconditional love, mainly because the love they display is the same pure love that God gives to each and every one of us.

They may not have the ability to clearly tell you about how much they love you or what they are thinking or feeling, but they are always completely honest about their feelings. It's a God-given gift that I know we all possess, if we would only use it.

Spunkie is a friend who has never let me down

and stands by my side no matter what the circumstances. Several times he's reminded me that I am not doing what he has learned in church. And on a few occasions he even told me I needed to talk to the Man Upstairs.

While discussing Christmas presents on the way to Wal-Mart one day, Spunkie informed me that Santa Claus would be coming soon, and we needed to be buying presents for everyone.

Santa Claus, one of Spunkie's best friends, had stopped by our house for a visit a few days earlier. He said he had been out checking on a few kids in our neighborhood and was on his way back to the North Pole. He told Spunkie he was pleased with the way he had kept his promises for the past year.

Santa took the opportunity in Spunkie's presence to turn his attention on me. "Mr. Balliew," he said, "you haven's kept the first promise you made me last year. I hear you've been acting like that old Grinch again. Instead of enjoying Christmas shopping, you always seem to be in a hurry, complaining about the long lines, speeding recklessly around with your shopping cart and bumping into people and things, I understand. I want you to promise me something else

7

this year: I want you to let my pal Spunkie look around a little and buy some presents so that I won't have to bring so many to your house."

All I had time to say was, "Yes, sir." After Spunkie whispered in Santa's ear about what he wanted for Christmas, Santa hugged Spunkie's neck. Then he looked at me, pointed a finger and said, "I hope you remember to keep your promises this year." Santa then shook our hands and left for the North Pole.

A few days later, as the two of us entered Wal-Mart, I got my first warning from Spunkie: "You better do what Santa Claus says."

"What did he say? I don't remember," I asked.

"He said to let me buy some goodies," replied Spunkie. I realized that I was being asked to slow down and let him look. This was unusual for the boy. My buddy, who seldom makes requests, may have been thinking about the gifts he wanted to buy for his friends. It was definitely a confidence builder for Spunkie having Santa give me that advice.

I decided to give him time. I told him, "Well, you can have at it, my boy." That got a smile from him. I told him to find me if he had any questions, or if he found anything he liked. With a wide grin, my star was on his way.

Spunkie is mentally limited and has a severe speech impediment. Therefore, I am very protective of him. I began to worry about Spunkie walking around Wal-Mart by himself. I am always afraid he will get involved with someone who will not be able to understand him, and who might ridicule or tease him. In the past he has been called "retard," "stupid," "clown" and some even laughed at him while running away and calling him "sicko."

Those times hurt me deeply. I cannot even begin to understand how those times made him feel. I had seen tears in his eyes several times, but he never complained. Unable to stand the pressure, I decided to follow my pal from a distance.

Spunkie's first stop was in the housewares section. He was looking at picture frames. Several times he would look at a specific red frame, and look away as if he was in deep thought. I wondered what was on his mind, and what that small picture frame was all about.

Spunkie turned to a saleslady who happened to be walking by and asked, "How much is this picture?" Showing her some bills that I was not aware he had, he asked, "Can I buy with money?"

"What? I don't understand what you are saying," the saleslady replied while shaking her head. As I said, Spunkie has a severe speech impediment, but over the years I had learned to understand him pretty well, even at a distance, by reading his lips.

"Can I buy picture with my money?" he asked. The saleslady, who I am sure did not understand him, shook her head and said something else I couldn't understand, then turned and walked away.

He stayed there for a few seconds staring at the picture frame. Finally, he put it back in its place on the shelf and walked away. I was about to walk towards him to ask if there was something I could help him with, but I changed my mind and let him continue shopping on his own.

I knew the picture frame was something he had been thinking about. It was for someone he cared about. I knew he was wondering if he had enough money to purchase the picture frame; it bothered me that the saleslady did not understand him. It was something that he could say he bought all by himself and I understood that this was a point of pride with him.

I didn't let Spunkie get too far away. He went

toward the crafts center and vanished down an aisle. He reappeared and vanished down another aisle. I finally couldn't stand it any longer; I had to see what he was doing and if he had any questions.

When I found him and asked how he was doing, his nod and confident smile assured me he was doing just fine. He was looking for things Santa could bring as a surprise. After I decided he was doing alright, I told him I was going to the fast-food restaurant in the back of the store to get a Coke. I told him I would be waiting for him and when he got there we would eat dinner.

It seemed like an eternity waiting on my pal. I didn't know what he was getting himself into, or what was on his mind. But suddenly Mr. Shadow appeared around the corner with a wide smile that showed his pride and happiness.

I asked him if he found any gifts he was going to ask Santa to bring his friends. He just held up the red picture frame he had been looking at and one large purple silk rose.

We ordered lunch; while eating I asked him, "Okay pal, so tell me about the gifts you are going to buy. Who are they for?"

His soft-voiced reply to me was, "Santa Claus can't bring it to her in Heaven. I give my baseball picture to Mrs. Balliew at her grave when we go up to her grave. So she can look down from Heaven and see it all day."

Suddenly the place got totally quiet, at least to me. It was as if no one else existed on this earth except Spunkie and myself. I no longer heard the music playing or the people around us talking. I was shocked. I asked, "What did you say? What do you mean, son?"

(Mrs. Inez Balliew, my late wife and the lady who raised Spunkie, had died seven years earlier, a few days after Christmas.)

Looking me right in the eyes, he said, "I miss Mrs. Balliew a bunch. Do you miss Mrs. Balliew a bunch? I love Mrs. Balliew a bunch. Do you love Mrs. Balliew a bunch?"

His eyes were misty, and he was staring as if he was trying to focus on a distant object. He said, "Mrs. Balliew gone to heaven. I tell God at church I bring my baseball picture and her flowers to give it to Mrs. Balliew." Again he said, "I miss Mrs. Balliew a bunch. Do you miss Mrs. Balliew a bunch? I love Mrs. Balliew a bunch. Do you love Mrs. Balliew a bunch?"

My heart nearly stopped. This guy was not supposed to be doing or saying these kinds of things. All of a sudden his mental limitation and speech impediment were not an issue. I had no idea he understood or learned so much in church, especially the meaning of talking to God.

When Spunkie looked up at me and said, "Mrs. Balliew said baby Jesus was in Heaven. Mrs. Balliew always holds babies up in Heaven in her arms. Them babies love Mrs. Balliew a bunch and don't cry no more much. I love Mrs. Balliew a bunch. You love Mrs. Balliew a bunch? Mrs. Balliew will be proud of me playing baseball in her picture."

"You are absolutely right, pal. Everyone is proud of you, son, and everyone will like the picture and flower, too. I know Mrs. Balliew loves you and for sure will really be proud of you too." I couldn't believe how I was holding my emotions together.

Spunkie had never sounded so mature in his life. I always knew he was a caring person, but I never had an idea he thought this way.

Spunkie had heard discussions of the possibility of him being able to play on a special baseball team. I also knew he was proud of the baseball uniform he was given for a picture and allowed to keep as his own. I was lost for words.

I must have looked strange because Spunkie asked me if I was OK and was I going to eat my chicken hamburger in a hurry. He reached into his pocket to pull out his money. He asked me if he had enough money to pay for Mrs. Balliew's picture frame and flower. I assured him he had plenty of money.

Looking at Spunkie, I was suddenly overwhelmed with a feeling I can't explain. I told my pal maybe I should try to do what I promised Santa because his elves might be watching me. Because

Spunkie is an avid believer in Santa, it only takes mentioning Santa's name and he shows his Christmas spirit.

While waiting for my star to finish his lunch, I remembered a conversation I had with Santa one Christmas while he was waiting to talk with some children. We both agreed that the Lord, in his infinite wisdom, allowed man to conceive the idea of Santa. He knew little ones and some others are not mature enough to understand the miracles of our Maker.

However, they could relate to Santa as someone who grants wishes to those that are thinking about being on their best behavior, and Santa was someone they can talk to. As these little fellows begin to mature and question the existence of Santa, a person who can make wonderful things happen. At that time they begin to understand and believe in a Higher Being as the grantor of miracles to those who believe.

Spunkie broke my chain of thought when he said, "I am through with eating my hamburger; we finished and I pay for Mrs. Balliew's present."

On the way home, I asked Spunkie when he decided to buy Mrs. Balliew the picture frame and flowers. I got my nonstop answers in a flash. "Santa

Claus can't go and give Mrs. Balliew her baseball picture in Heaven. Can we wrap it up and give it on Mrs. Balliew grave on Christmas? Can we put it by a Christmas tree for her? Will Mrs. Balliew be happy? Can I put paper and a ribbon on it? Will you help me put my baseball picture in the picture? I love Mrs. Balliew a bunch. Do you love Mrs. Balliew a bunch? Will Santa Claus be proud of me?"

I slowed my Christmas shopper down when I said, "Tell you what, pal let's go up to see Mrs. Balliew right now. How about it, my boy?"

"Yep! But we don't tell her about my baseball picture surprise," replied Spunkie.

When we arrived at Mrs. Balliew's grave, the sun was a brilliant orange and was just setting. Beautiful shadows were already lengthening, bringing back favorite memories of the many times the three of us had stood in this same spot, with Inez and me planning our times to be together in this final resting place.

It also made me think of how she held a nonverbal, mentally-limited 8-year-old's hand while she told him about Jesus and how He could see us here. How when we died we would be placed here and we could come and visit each other. How that Jesus would

16

look out for us until we all got to heaven. So many important things in Spunkie's life were discussed here in Chandler Cemetery.

I thought of the time she held him in her lap and told him that Christmas was the time we needed to remember baby Jesus. Baby Jesus, Mrs. Balliew told him, was the reason we gave the people we love Christmas presents.

We stood there without speaking for a few moments. Spunkie broke the silence by saying, "Mrs. Balliew is up in Heaven holding babies who can fly up in the air and plays around all the time. She holds little babies who don't feel good and make them better. She tells babies not to cry no more and they feel better again."

"How do you know that, pal?" I asked.

"The preacher said at church about angels and baby Jesus. You say Mrs. Balliew is in Heaven and Mrs. Balliew is angel. I see Mrs. Balliew sometimes when she looks like a angel. I love Mrs. Balliew a bunch. Do you love Mrs. Balliew a bunch?"

I stood there as humble as I have ever been in my life. I didn't know what to say or think. I reached over and hugged my best buddy for a few seconds.

"Spunkie, Mrs. Balliew and I are proud of you. We love you a ton, son. We are definitely going to give Mrs. Balliew her Christmas present. And we are definitely going to get her a Christmas tree for you to put your baseball picture and purple flower by." We left after telling Mrs. Balliew we loved her and were quiet most of the way home.

I was not allowed to forget Mrs. Balliew's Christmas tree. One day Spunkie practically demanded, "We go buy a Christmas tree to take to Mrs. Balliew's grave because Santa Claus comes here real soon."

We looked in several stores for the perfect tree; we made sure to always purchase a few ornaments from each store. We finally bought a small artificial tree. We spent several enjoyable evenings decorating the tree, and discussing the day we would place the tree at Mrs. Balliew's grave and how proud she would be of my buddy.

After we finished decorating the tree I will have to admit it looked absolutely wonderful sitting on our kitchen table for a few days. Spunkie asked several times if this was the day we were going to take it and put it at Mrs. Balliew's grave so she could look down and see it. I told Spunkie, when he finished wrapping

18

the baseball picture we would take them both and put them at Mrs. Balliew's grave at the same time.

After he tried several times to wrap the picture he never could get it wrapped the way he wanted it to look. I asked him if he wanted me to wrap it for him. He shook his head and said, "Can I put my baseball picture at Mrs. Balliew's grave now? She can't see it from Heaven with a bunch of paper all on it." I was really surprised he had decided that by himself.

I told him that it was his present for Mrs. Balliew and he could give it to her any way he wanted to. Then he said, "I don't put paper on her flower so she can see it too down from Heaven," looking at me as if I might object.

"Wonderful, buddy," I told him.

The next evening I noticed Spunkie sitting at the kitchen table holding the picture and looking at the tree when he asked, "Can we take the Christmas tree and her picture to Mrs. Balliew now?"

"You better believe it pal, but let's wait until later to take the baseball picture, OK? It might get wet if it rains," I said.

"She won't see my baseball picture from Heaven until later?" Spunkie asked with a sad look.

"Do you want to take them both now?" I asked. I got a positive nod, so we gathered the Christmas gifts and a poinsettia wreath we had purchased earlier, placed them in the car and started towards Chandler Cemetery. When we were almost there Spunkie jumped and said, "We forgot it, Mr. Balliew, we forgot it."

"Forgot what, pal?"

"We forgot the flower, Mrs. Balliew's flower, we forgot it, we got to go back to get it," Spunkie said, and I turned around to retrieve Mrs. Balliew's flower.

When we arrived at the cemetery, we didn't speak a word to each other but went about our work putting the tree close to our marker and placing the picture on the ledge. With the purple rose in his hand Spunkie said, "Mrs. Balliew's flower is beautiful, Mrs. Balliew likes pretty flowers, and she will like my pretty flower when she looks down from Heaven."

All of a sudden it hit me and the tears began. I had thought very little about the rose. We had placed it out of sight and hadn't discussed it during the time we decorated the tree and discussed the picture. The baseball picture, the tree, the rose, and the desire of a mentally challenged loved one and his memory had overwhelmed me. His desire to show someone he loved dearly, that he still thought of her was bigger than my heart could handle. I believe he still remembered how much Mrs. Balliew loved this time of year.

I was recalling the memories of how we came together as a family, and especially how much time she spent with Spunkie. I know that, at that moment, both Spunkie and I felt her love, the same love we felt when she was there. I looked at Spunkie and saw that he had tears in his eyes, too. I hugged his neck and told him how happy Mrs. Balliew must feel right now and how much she loved him for thinking of her at Christmas.

As we started to leave I looked at the inscriptions on our marker and thought, "Mama, me and your boy sure do love you, and he is our bright star because you took the time to teach him to shine. No one knows better than you, honey, how far he has come since the days you held his hand as an 8-year-old little fellow in a diaper, who had seizures almost everyday, who couldn't talk and knew nothing about personal hygiene. I can't hear you say it but I know exactly what you are saying at this moment.

"I know you would hug our necks like you always did. I know you would tell Spunkie how much the Christmas tree, flower and his baseball picture mean to you. I know you would tell Spunkie how handsome he looks in his baseball uniform, and we would share smiles of love knowing how much your praise means to him."

I caught myself saying aloud, "Merry Christmas, Mama. Me and the boy sure do love and miss you more than you know."

I know stars represent the highest ideals and hopes of mankind. To be a star means one has accomplished, has attained, has aspired to something beyond the normal range of ability and responsibility. Stars sometimes twinkle, and then fade; some stars continue to shine forever. All are filled with life and light for a purpose.

Spunkie Keener is a star that has and will forever shine. He found a way to share a Christmas message of love for a person he knows taught him what love feels like. Scottie "Spunkie" Keener gave God's gift. He found what most of us never find: he found how to share God's true love while feeling it himself. He gave himself.

I know if Mrs. Balliew was here she would do as she did many times before: kiss Spunkie on the cheek and say, "Thank you, honey. Merry Christmas and I love you." I truly believe Mrs. Balliew is an angel who is carrying out the Lord's will. Angels can do anything, I understand—maybe she already has.

I've seen Spunkie quietly standing and staring at our Christmas tree, smiling, with his hand on his cheek. Merry Christmas, Mama, I love you.

Deacon Balliew and His Winner's Club

by Roy Exum
Staff writer for the *Chattanooga News-Free Press*

One day, Deacon Balliew was approached about starting a Cub Scout den for some mentally challenged kids in Calhoun, Georgia. He was a little leery of such a deal, so he decided to test himself.

He took three of the boys, ages 10, 16, and 20, in his car and picked up a bag of groceries. Off to the woods they went for a weenie roast. Late that night when he got home, he put his arms around his wife, Inez, and said quietly, "We aren't going to start a Cub Scout pack for kids of this age—we're going to start a Boy Scout troop."

It might have been at that very moment that the "Legend of Deacon Balliew" began. And that's the way it's been ever since—with Deacon searching for children to love.

The toughest part back then—as well as today— is convincing folks that God made all of us, and he doesn't make any mistakes," explains Deacon. "And this is for certain: we can all be winners at something."

On the basis of that principle, his Scouts thrived. One could tie knots quicker then anybody else. Another could build the best campfire. Still another could run faster. And at tug-o-war those boys, working together, were all winners.

They went to Boy Scout Camporees and summer camp competitions—and won. Soon they were one of the best Scout troops around and were personally invited, merit badges and all, to the White House by the Commander in Chief, Jimmy Carter..

"We tried to prepare for it," Deacon grins at the memory of that afternoon., "but when the President comes out on that grass and wraps his arms around you... man, that's the big time!"

But that was nothing, absolutely zero, compared with what Deacon and Inez have done for hundreds of kids since.

Welcome to The Winner's Club, which Deacon calls a "place of dreams." Here he, in his very special way, can indeed light a candle in the darkness of the mind.

Once a boy confided to Deacon that he wanted to play high school football in the very worst way. That was his dream. And it was Deacon who led the cheers when the boy, who tried so very hard, learned he had enough playing time to wear his letter jacket. "Is the kid retarded?" Deacon was asked.

In a quiet voice, he answered simply, "Let's just say he is a member of The Winner's Club."

The clubhouse had humble beginnings, starting out as an old storage shed. The new building has not a penny owing on it and features bathrooms with rails, so the handicapped can move around with grace. There are low kitchen counters; even the littlest club members can reach the cereal and milk, grab a cookie and—best of all—learn to function for themselves.

Michael, a 12 year old, started coming to the club when it was learned he had an inoperable brain tumor. "One day," recalls Deacon, "we had been working alongside each other for a while, and finally I asked him, 'Michael, you ever have a dream?' That boy looked at me and said, 'I've never seen the ocean,' and I asked him if he's like to go. Well, he brightened up considerably and I put it in the back of my mind to get him there.

"I mentioned the deal to Michael's mother, and not too long afterward she took him to a doctor in Atlanta. On the way back home, she stopped to call me. 'Deacon,' she said, 'if you are taking Michael to the beach... you have to go now.'"

By the time his mother had driven Michael the rest of the way home, Balliew had lined up an airplane, a pilot, a deep sea charter boat, a hotel, and Michael's doctor to be available by phone in case he was needed. Several weeks later, when Michael died, Deacon hugged the boy's mother for a long time and handed her pictures of Michael, laughing and shouting in the surf.

The Winner's Club—it is a place of dreams. And

the gentle Balliew had the first one.

Deacon Balliew, originally named William, was born the son of a cotton mill operator in Calhoun, 1937. He loved music and soon found himself playing guitar in a rock 'n roll band in Atlanta. But he says the best thing that came out of that, was when he was dazzled by a girl named Inez on a street corner during a parade.

The band was being booked in some tough places, one so tough a net of chicken wire had to be installed to protect the musicians from flying beer bottles, so he and Inez, now with a baby, moved on. After a couple of years they traveled to Dallas, where Balliew went to college for a short time. Then he decided to learn to be a bowling alley mechanic, and he went north for training. "One day I quoted some Scripture, and people started calling me 'The Southern Deacon.' That nickname stuck like glue."

The couple, by now with their second child on the way, went to live in Deacon's beloved Calhoun, Balliew working in the carpet mills. The world began to blossom when Deacon became enraptured by kids, especially those who were shy, uncoordinated, small or weak. "I found myself, for the first time in my life," he

29

says with a slight smile.

He would play tee ball with kids none of the other coaches seemed to want—the slighted kids, ones with beat up knees, kids who desperately clutched tattered, third generation gloves. "When a boy would hide behind his mama or look ready to cry, I'd be interested," he admits.

What Deacon taught those little ballplayers was the will to win. He would take his team out to center field just before the game and say, "Fellas, the only folks you'll be with out there are your pals. If you all work together, we may get beat—but we will not lose!"

After that came the Scouts, and then The Winner's Club, which was at first little more then a "grown up" version of those ball teams and Scout groups. And girls were included, too.

So today Deacon and Inez take the weak, the infirm, those with steel braces on their legs, and they help them become winners. Like the boy who whispered to his beloved Balliew that he wanted to run in some races. He knew he was fast, but he couldn't run on the high school team because...well, just because.

So Deacon, who in his quiet way had helped get

30

the Special Olympics started in Gordon County, practiced with that boy two or three times a week. For three years they worked together. Jackie Proctor breezed through local, state and regional competition. Next came the internationals, in faraway Brockport, NY, and Jackie made it to the finals of the 200 meters. Deacon remembers holding his breath when Jackie lined up with the other finalists for a once in a lifetime dash to greatness.

Muhammad Ali was there that afternoon, and Jackie showed the champ, along with several thousand other cheering people, that three years spent on that lonely track, sometimes rainy and cold, were part of a dream. Jackie Proctor was absolutely untouchable.

"Those kids can't help that fate dealt them a tough hand, that they were born mentally handicapped or that they've been abused. They can't help that. But here's somebody," Deacon thumbs his chest, "who can."

Inez and Deacon, their own children long since grown, got custody last November of an eight year old who had worn diapers all his life and rarely spoke. One day last winter, that boy jumped out of Deacon's van, ran into the house, and used the bathroom, all on his own. The next morning he hugged Deacon and said, "Bye, I love you, Mr. Balliew..."

Deacon cried all the way to work.

Balliew remembers a little girl who would run every time she saw a stranger. Today that girl, who turned out to be an exceptional student once she overcame her horrible shyness, has been accepted at Reinhardt College in Waleska, Georgia.

Not long after The Winner's Club was formed, a judge talked Deacon into working with the Gordon County Juvenile Court on a full-time basis. Today, as Balliew drives through town, he must do so with one hand; he is busy waving at nearly everybody with the other.

"I can truly say that when the Lord takes me out of this world, I'll be happy," says Deacon. "Some people play golf, others dabble in the stock market, but me, I spend every minute I can with the kids. I can tell you right now what I'll be doing the day I die."

He will be helping kids like Charlie. Charlie was doing fine until a horrible car collision sent him flying head first through the windshield. A lot of folks said Charlie would "never be right" again. Deacon Balliew was not one of them.

As he nurtured Charlie along, he discovered the boy could sing like nobody he had ever known. So Deacon's dream for Charlie was to cut an album. Included among the songs was a gospel hymn called, "Sweet Beulah Land."

Even the hardest heart will soften when a stunning chorus of about 50 other children joins in. Only later, when you see the tears form in Deacon's eyes as he hears the recording, do you realize that the chorus is made up entirely of kids from The Winner's Club.

Today the same Charlie travels a long way from Calhoun, singing in the "big time," while Deacon and Inez look over about 50 kids just like him at the clubhouse.

Asked what is important in dealing with children, Deacon's answer is quick. "Don't ever tell a lie." He pauses. "And help them find their dreams.

Michael's Dash

We have all seen our share of tombstones. But like most people I seldom took time to remember any of the small notations placed on them by their loved ones. Usually underneath the name there will be a birth date, a dash, and the date the loved one left the family and friends

Since a child I have always been told that the most important part of any tombstone was the dash.

We have all seen the names of people, the day they were born and the day they died which we will most times forget. But the dash on each tombstone—that between the beginning and the end—is what represents that individual's time here with us. And if it's remembered and recorded and passed on, it represents a part of a person's life that will always last.

My grandmother told me many times that everybody needed to be on a straight and narrow path because people will forget the day you were born and the day you died, but if you lived like God wanted you to, they will never forget your dash.

I'm going to share a dash with you that I will never forget. It was a dash that helped place me on a path for which I will always be grateful.

He was short and stocky, with brown hair combed so not one hair was out of place, and he had dark blue eyes. He was really a good-looking 13-year-old kid. His features were swollen from the medication, as his mother had warned me.

He was wearing jeans and a sporty long-sleeved shirt. He always wore this one hat: it was black in back and red in the front, with an Atlanta Falcons logo. I rarely saw him without it.

I immediately knew he was the kind of kid I would like, all smiles with a happy, kind of excited voice. I saw how he related to other Winners Club kids who also saw what I did. And as always at the Winners Club, none of them saw his handicap; they just saw another kid. The girls later told me they all thought he was cute. I believe that, because the girls did the "giggle thing" they always did when a handsome young man was around.

After a couple of Thursday meetings, I went to see Michael's mother to get any advice she could share with me. She told me that Michael was happy and enjoyed the Winners Club and the kids. She also told me the details of the medical problems that Michael was facing. He had an inoperable brain tumor and through her tears also told me that it was terminal. The doctors in Marietta had told her he had only a few months to live.

As I was driving home I said my first prayer which was simply, "Pal, I'm really going to need your help to deal with every one of these inadequate feelings I have and I'm going to need you to help me to understand Michael and his feelings." You can believe me when I tell you the Lord came through in many wonderful ways. That period of my life was the time God showed me that He will answer prayers, when you ask and believe.

One of the first things that young fellow taught me was a special skill he had developed: the ability to make me feel at ease around him. He could find something for us to talk about that was usually funny. He could not stand it if I seemed sad or down.

If you were sad around him, chances were you wouldn't be sad for very long. Making people happy was very easy for him to do, because he was always so happy. I only remember one time that I saw him said. It amazed me how everyone was always so happy around him; that's just the kind of guy that he was, I guess.

When he was around people that he didn't know too well, he didn't talk very much and he was pretty calm and quiet. After they got to know him, and he got to know them, he relaxed and became his normal wild and crazy self.

Most of the time he was honest, but sometimes, when he told you something that he thought would bother you, he would bend the story just a little so no one's feelings were hurt. No matter what, he seemed to always find something funny to talk about when I needed a good friend.

Along with loving to be with and around people, he loved sports. He was very good at just about every sport, but he was the best at fishing. He loved fishing. Every day after school he would go outside and practice casting with his rod and reel for hours at a time. He was a kid who could daydream out loud, and he was very good at catching imaginary fish.

I admired how he was so devoted to his practice sessions, and how he was so good at it. I also admired how much he cared for his friends, his family, and just everyone that he was around. I wasn't the only one who admired him, either. Everyone that I knew talked

38

about how sweet he was. When I saw his teachers at school or in town they always complimented him on the way he was handling his trouble.

Even though he was always happy on the outside, he was not so happy with how some people treated him. I think he treated everyone so well because he knew how it felt not to be treated well. He cared about everyone and everything except for the few that made fun of him, and it hurt me to see such a nice, caring kid feel bad. He helped me get over my self-esteem problem, and I wish I realized it at the time and told him about it.

I remember one night we were just hanging out doing some work and having a good time, when he asked if he could try his hand at making something on the wood lathe. I had hoped he would ask because I had a piece of wood all ready to install in the machine. He finally got the hang of it, and before long he had an 18-inch baseball bat—or that is what he said it looked like to him. I noticed something else that evening also: two fellows realizing they were getting to be buddies.

We were just sitting there in the shop talking, when he told me there was something that he didn't think I knew about him: that he was sick and one day he might have to go to the hospital for a long time and he might die. He also mentioned that last year he had been taken to the hospital a few times, because he had a tumor.

I started to get really worried. I told him that his mother had told me something about that, but none of his pals in the club had noticed and I sure hadn't. That's when he told me in a way that only he could. I get emotional faster than the average person, and I'm a lot slower in dealing with this kind of thing.

He simply said, "But you don't have to worry none; I ain't." I thought I had known him really well, but right then I knew we were pals forever.

We spent several evenings around that old Craftsman wood lathe that a buddy, J.C. Maddox, had given the Club a few years back. Even all these years later, I still see it in storage and remember vividly our discussions about his desires and dreams.

When I heard what he told me that evening, it was fantastic; it made me care more about him. He made me realize a friend is a valuable thing and you should like them for what they are and not their situation.

It wasn't because he was sick, even though he

was. Instead, it was because he was a valuable person that made this old boy do a lot of soul searching and a lot more praying than what I had done in the past.

Over the next few weeks Michael and I had the opportunity to go fishing at some of the local lakes and ponds. He always amazed me the way he could cast the rod and reel. "Like a pro," I told him.

One day we were sitting and waiting for the fish to bite when I asked him what he dreamed about doing. The answer was quick. He said he had seen the fishing shows on TV and wished he could fish like that. "But," he said, "I would be afraid to ride a fast boat. I saw one wreck one time on TV and the man got hurt bad."

I told him that I had a buddy named Billy Bearden who had a boat like the ones on TV, and he was also a champion fisherman just like the ones he saw on the television. I told Michael how he fished with all of the "big time TV fishermen."

I told Michael I would ask Billy about going fishing with him. Michael asked me not to do it because he would be afraid, and that's when I told him about "Slow Poke" Bearden, as the big time fisherman called him. He was called "Slow Poke" because all the other fishermen had to go around him on their way to catch fish.

"Man, does he really go that slow?" Michael asked. After that it was all right for me to ask about a fishing trip, since we would be going at a slow enough speed for Michael. When I asked Billy, he agreed to take Michael fishing at Lake Weiss in Alabama and that he would keep the "Slow Poke" tale in mind.

He mentioned that he hadn't had any dealing with a kid with a terminal illness and said he would be nervous. I told Billy that I had learned something: just treat him just like any other kid you take fishing.

Billy definitely could handle that. He had spent several years of his life working with kids as director of the Calhoun, Georgia Recreation Department.

When the big day arrived Michael and I met Billy. I was glad I told him about being a "Slow Poke" because the first question out of Michael's mouth was "Mr. Bearden, is your nickname Slow Poke Billy?"

Billy answered, "Did Deacon tell you that?"

"Yep!"

"Well, if your friend Deacon told you that, then I guess he should know."

We got the boat off the trailer, the fishing gear stored in place, life preservers on, the motor started and eased out of the loading area. *WHAM!* The nose of the boat stood straight up. The front of Michael's hair looked like it was glued to his scalp by the wind. (I was lucky to get a picture of it.)

When Billy slowed down, Michael looked at me with a frown on his face and said, "Boy! All of them other fishermen must be crazy! You told me Billy was Mr. Slow Poke. What do they call them other fishermen? Mr. Rocket Men?"

We all got a good laugh, especially Michael, when he realized that "Slow Poke" was a safe boat driver anyway. We had a fantastic day thanks to Billy, and caught fish, too! (Billy and I have relived that day several times in the past few years.)

One of the fish Michael caught at Lake Weiss we took to a friend, Billy Elphingstone, who let Michael watch as he mounted it for him. Later I told him that his fish looked good enough to eat. He told me it was too small. We would have to go to the ocean to catch one big enough for me to eat.

I asked him if he had ever been deep-sea fishing. He answered, "Nope! But I wish I could go and see the ocean, too."

"Maybe some day we can go there."

"You promise?" he asked.

"We will see," I said.

"That sounds like a promise to me, buddy," he said.

I thought about taking him to the ocean and I discussed it with his mother. It had been several months since we met. After each visit to the doctor, when I looked at his mother's face I knew things weren't getting any better.

They were going to start a medication that could probably help relieve the bouts of headaches. For a few weeks the medication seemed to be helping, but the problems seemed to be getting worse and it was back to the doctors at the Shriners' Hospital again.

**

I will never forget that phone call. I was working at my office in the Gordon County Juvenile Court when I answered the phone. It was Michael's mother telling me that the doctors had told her that if we were going to take Michael to the ocean, we had better hurry.

I sat there in shock. And I guess I looked like it; a coworker of mine, Jackie McEntyre, asked, "Deacon, what's the matter with you? You look like you've seen a ghost."

When I told her about the phone call, everyone in the office had tears in their eyes. We all knew about Michael's condition, what the phone call was about and we all loved Michael.

What was I going to do about the promise I had made to Michael? Sitting there at my desk, Michael's mother's words kept ringing in my ears: "The doctor said if you are going to take Michael to see the ocean you had better hurry."

I quietly sat there at the desk and called on the Lord again, "Pal, I am asking for Your help big time again. You haven't failed to help in the past, and I sure need You now with these plans and decisions all of us will have to make. And Pal, take care of my little buddy, too. Lord, you know how scared I am so please help me."

I began to think of the people who in the past had believed in the Winners Club and always had ideas and help when there was a need. Tommy Brown, J.C. Maddox, John Wayne Hall, Clarence Harris, George Caron, Sheriff Pat Baker, Sam Thomas, and others.

I was very lucky: all of them were in their offices when I called. I told them Michael's story and the need to be in a hurry. (We have a policy at the Winners Club to never discuss why a person had been referred to us or what difficulties he or his family faces, but this time was the exception.)

The ideas and financial help began to come in fast. Tommy Brown knew of a motel in Panama City, Florida, and gave me the contact person's name and phone number to call.

John Wayne Hall knew of a fishing charter service in Destin, Florida, and gave me the phone number and captain of the boat to contact.

Sheriff Pat Baker called back and told me our

friend Bill Akins had agreed to fly us down there and knew the manager of a car rental service that he was sure would have a car ready for us.

I called another pilot friend, Dr. Verne Dortch. He owned a plane and had helped with our kids in the past, and he agreed to help fly us there. He also agreed to contact Michael's doctor for any suggestions about Michael's medical conditions and would be in contact with Bill Akins and make the trip arrangements.

***

I will never in my life forget the caring I felt from people that day, especially when Jackie McEntyre walked over to my desk handed me a check for $300. She couldn't hide her emotions; she just looked at me with tears in her eyes and said "here" and walked out of the office for a while.

I called Michael's mother and told her what was happening and to tell Michael to be ready tomorrow afternoon for his fishing trip. She asked me to tell Michael because she probably would leave out a few details. All I remember telling him was about the trip and that I planned to catch a bigger fish than him, even if I had to find a way to cheat.

"How can anybody cheat fishing?" he asked.

"I don't know, but I'll find a way if I have to. I just know I can't let a kid beat me at fishing."

I also told him before we hung up the phone, "Remember to say a prayer for me and my bigger fish."

"You bet I won't," he said and laughed.

Michael's mother's had called me at 2:15 in the afternoon. I left the office at 5:00 PM knowing we were about ready to go. We had $3,500 in donations, hotel reservations, a chartered fishing boat, and a lady captain ready to take us out ocean fishing, two trusted pilots and a plane to fly us there, a rental car ready at Panama City airport, and a doctor standing by just in case.

***

I couldn't believe all that had happened in two hours and 45 minutes. On the way home I looked up toward the sky and said, "Thanks, Pal. Lord, as always You came through again. Thanks for all that's happening and all that is going to happen."

The next morning I talked with Michael's mother. I told her that today was going to be a big day in our buddy's life.

She told me Michael hardly slept last night and that he would be there on time. It was hard to believe that less than 24 hours ago all this started and we were

48

on our way to the local airport.

I had decided to record an audiocassette for Michael to listen to after the trip. That recording has meant more to me and his family than anyone can imagine. I have listened to it many times in the past 25 years and am amazed at the new things I hear each time I listen to it—and how a terminally ill young fellow could develop an understanding about his fate and comfort the ones around him.

Dr. Dortch and Bill Akins were already at the airport and were busy filing the flight plans and making sure all was ready for the trip to Panama City. Soon Michael arrived wearing the same familiar Falcons football cap that I had come to know. He was sporting a new pair of overalls that he said were just like the ones I wore a lot.

Before we boarded the plane, Bill Akins, for all our sakes, went over all the things that would be happening on our flight and the things for Michael to be looking out for, what we would experience and hear.

He was calming Michael's fears, because he knew Michael had never been in a plane before. We all boarded the plane and finally we were in the air. A large group of friends and family members had come to the

49

airport to see Michael off on his Florida fishing trip and all were waving when we went out of sight. It seemed like Michael would have sprained his neck the way he kept looking back and waving.

All of a sudden we were in the first of many clouds on that trip and our edgy passenger made the first grab at his seat belt harness—making white knuckles on his left hand. When he did finally relax and lower his hand, any turbulence, clouds, the plane's radio, someone coughing or waking up from a catnap caused him to grab the harness and get white-knuckled again.

When I explained to him about the white knuckles and why he got all white-knuckled, he said, "I won't fall out that way; have you looked down there yet? It's a long way down there."

That was when Bill told him we were a mile-and-a-half up in the air. I saw another sudden move to that white-knuckled grip again.

We had several discussions while in the air, which usually centered on his blowing off my doors fishing, that our boat captain was a lady and how I was going to be the biggest gentleman of the two of us. That way she would help me catch the biggest fish, so I wouldn't have to find a way to cheat.

I told him that I for sure wouldn't want to go back home and have to tell everyone that a certain kid had beaten me fishing.

About that time Dr. Dortch told him we were going 190 miles an hour and were one and a half miles up. He looked out the window, I think for the last time, and you guessed it: white knuckles again.

I had noticed our fisherman several times getting an envelope out of the bib of his overalls, and each time he got it out he looked at me with a look that said, "Ask me about this." I finally couldn't stand it any longer and ask, "What you got in that envelope, pal?"

With a smile he said, "$50.00 to spend any way I want too. Mama and them told me I might need it to buy some snacks and stuff. When we can, I want stop and buy some stuff."

I suggested, "Man you sure got a wad of money there and I think someone who knows a lot about snacks and stuff needs to help you spend that wad of loot.

All I heard was, "Bull" as the envelope was stored away in the overall bib.

"Hey look at the ocean down there, it sure is the

biggest swimming pool I have ever see, I can't wait to take what you call 'a refreshing dip' in it." an excited Michael said.

Bill and Doctor Dortch, our pilots, told us that we were nearing Panama City and that got his attention. White-knuckle time came once more as we made our descent and landed.

We left Calhoun at approximately 2:15 p.m. and arrived in Panama City at 5 p.m. Our boy needed to know if that was going as fast as a racecar. Our rental car was ready and shortly we were on our way to the hotel.

My friend who made the arrangements, Tommy Brown, must have known the owner because we had a fantastic room with a view to match. Michael had seen the ocean from the plane the few times he looked out.

When he looked out the hotel window, he threw on his bathing suit in a flash and hurried me up so he could take a refreshing dip in "the world's biggest swimming hole" I had been kidding him about.

In the next 30 minutes he couldn't stop talking: about the hot white sand, the clear warm water, coming back tonight, fishy smelling air, waves chasing him to shore, rip tides his cousin told him about, pretty girls

52

supposed to be down here, his hat blowing off too much and would I hold it, fast long legged birds, and having fun.

He was not a happy camper though when he had to take the shower to get the sand off. The water was like ice, and "could make my lips turn blue" and "might make my brain start to freeze like ice cream does sometimes," he said.

Back in the room we made the phone call to this family that we had promised, so he could report to everyone about what he was doing. It took him about 15 minutes to recap the trip thus far, and especially the beach. He told about the adjoining room we shared with Bill and Dr. Dortch and the supper that they had planned at a great big boat and all he was going to eat was shrimp, fish, hushpuppies and all the Coke he could drink, and then he was going to order a dessert and didn't know what it would be yet.

The adjoining room that Dr. Dortch and Bill shared gave them an opportunity to share in Michael's excitement. Michael was now at ease and comfortable with all three of us, and that was wonderful.

We went to dinner at Captain Anderson's Restaurant, which looked like a big pirate ship, and the

53

boy kept his word. He ate 38 shrimp, some fish and even was accused of stealing two of Bill's hushpuppies. I don't know about the Coke, but the dessert was a giant piece of chocolate cake with icing a half-inch thick.

He was putting away his napkin when he said, "I'm ready to hit the swimming hole again." So, we were on our way to have another dip.

On the way to the hotel our young man with the burning overall pocket said, "Can we stop and buy some goodies to snack on for our room?

Bill said he thought there was a convenience close to our hotel, and he would stop there so Michael could cool off the burning pocket I was talking about. While in the store Michael ask me if I wanted any snacks and agreed to buy them.

I said, "Thanks Pal, I want a six pack of coke, box of those crackers, a box of that chocolate candy on the top shelf, and brown cow ice cream to munch on while on the way to the hotel."

"Bull, I ain't got no million dollars to spend on that much stuff. If you eat that much stuff you will get sick," our boy said.

"I guess you're right, Buddy lets wait. I need to

be in good shape in the morning; I got work to do." I said with a smile.

It was 9 o'clock at night and the beach was completely deserted. From one of the beach chairs I watched a kid having the time of his life running, jumping waves, and hollering at me to look at how high he could jump… when all of a sudden a large wave came from out of nowhere, knocking him down and covering him completely.

He made his highest jump at that instant, coming up coughing and spitting, and ran out of the water. He said, "This is the most fun I had so far, playing in the ocean at night."

I asked him why he jumped up so fast and ran when the wave hit him. He said, "It hit me hard and scared me to death. I swallowed a lot of water and thought I was going to be in one of them rip tides."

I asked him where he had heard about rip tides and he informed me that a cousin had told him that rip tides would knock you down and suck you out into the ocean where a whale or some big giant fish might eat you up. I told him that hearing a tale like that scared me, too, and I thought it was time to go to the room and hit the sack.

Just like the night before the shower was another treat for me; he put on a jumping show when that cold shower hit him. He warned me that his lips would turn blue if he stayed in it too long.

We finally got into bed about 10:30 and he told me that he was having a bunch of fun. He then said, "Mr. Balliew, I sure hope my mother is not worried about me being so far away from home."

"I don't think so, pal. You've talked to her and told her everything is OK," I said.

Then he asked, "Do you ever worry about anything?"

I asked him, "Boy, have you ever heard of a worry wart?"

He said, "Yep! My sister calls me one all the time."

"Well," I told him, "they named the real worry wart after me because that is how much I worry sometimes."

I asked him if he ever worried.

"Yep, I sure do; what worries me all the time is mama and the others worrying about me being sick and going to die. I know I am going to Heaven when I die and they don't need to worry all the time. I hear them

56

crying, and it scares me."

Suddenly I felt small and scared. I thought "Help me to say the right thing, Lord." I told him, "You know buddy, a kid like you has been chosen by God and Jesus to come to Heaven because He needed you for something special and besides, you know you are going to be around the best fisherman that has ever been in the world."

"Jesus," he said.

"You guessed it, pal. His name is Jesus, and He must have looked down here and saw you and decided that you were exactly the kind of kid He needed for that special job. You will probably be some kind of angel. And will you do me a favor, old pal, when you get to see and talk to Jesus; I want you to tell him to look down here. You will have to point at me so He will know me and ask Him to be sure to let me catch the biggest fish every time and not to have to look for a way to cheat to win."

He giggled and said, "You crazy or something? I'm gonna tell him to let you catch minnows."

Also, I told him, "You know, Jesus has a large group of fishermen that He hangs out with, called disciples. They helped Him all the time, and I would bet since you can fish so well you might be in that crowd, too."

He was quiet for a few seconds and said, "Mr. Balliew, I'm sure glad we are buddies, and I love you, too."

"We sure are best friends and buddies, and I love you too, pal," I told him.

"Yep, and Mr. Balliew, don't tell my mother and them. I'm worried about them because it might worry them."

I winked at him, nodded my head, and said, "You got my promise, buddy."

He looked up at me with his wide sleepy eyes, winked, and said, "Winking at each other will always mean we are keeping our promises and secrets, and we are buddies."

I winked back and said, "You got that right, little man." He winked again as he covered himself. It was 11:45 p.m. and our tired fisherman was asleep in seconds.

Before I went to sleep, I asked the Lord to give me the strength and knowledge to say and do the right things the next day. I also thanked him for my family, Michael, Billy, Dr. Dortch and all the friends that had caused me to see one of His miracles in progress. And I asked Him to help me understand my feelings and to keep me from being so scared and worried.

That was over twenty-five years ago and I remember that night like it was last night.

We were up at 5:30 the next morning. Michael went to the window and saw that it was still dark and said, "Why are we up when it is still dark? You can't catch fish in the dark."

I told him one of my ways to beat a kid fishing was not to let him sleep too much, so maybe he would go to sleep on the boat and not catch any fish. He just looked at me, frowned, and said, "I ain't going to sleep on no boat; I'm staying awake all the time so I can watch you. I'll tell Mr. Bill and Dr. Dortch to help me keep a lookout, too."

I could tell my pal was not a morning person.

I asked him if he had brought any cats down with him. He just looked at me with that same frown and his not-awake-yet look and said, "No! Why?"

I told him, "I thought I heard what sounded like two cats fighting in your bed. I've never in my life heard so much snorting, howling, snoring, screeching, grunting, whining and other cat-fighting sounds in my

59

life. Did you hear them?"

"No, I was asleep."

"I don't see how any kid could sleep with cats fighting in bed with them."

He smiled and said, "I thought you was for real."

"I was for real. Something sounded like cats fighting in your bed," I told him. "What are you going to eat for breakfast, more shrimp and chocolate cake?" And that is when I saw that "look" again.

He said, "Boy, I ain't never going to eat no shrimp and chocolate cake again."

I told him, "I don't blame you. That was probably your belly saying 'Please don't eat any more shrimp and cake!' that made it sound like cats fighting in bed with you."

"Yeah," he said. I winked at him and he said instantly, "You better not tell," and gave me a halfhearted wink.

I asked him if he was going to take a shower and was quickly informed he took his last night in "cold" water and didn't think he needed another one.

I then asked, "Are you a betting man? How much money have you got left, and do you want to bet me money you can beat me fishing?"

60

He told me as if he had already planned it: "No, I'm buying me a boat with paddle holes and some more stuff with my money. I'm ready to go catch the biggest fish so you will be sad."

Bill and Doc were at the car waiting. Away we went to McDonald's for pancakes, and then went to the docks in Destin. We found our lady captain and her boat at 7:30 a.m. and what a fantastic greeting.

She already knew about Michael. I never did find out how she had gotten so much information. She immediately took Michael under her guidance, and away we went.

The fishing was not as good as we had hoped. Each time we got a bite Michael would make a dash for the pole, except the time he had to use the bathroom. We got a bite and I pulled in one that I couldn't believe got his mouth open wide enough to get hooked. It was only about as long as my hand.

All of the other fish had been thrown back into the ocean. I told the captain to put this one in the well. When Michael got back, I told him to look in the well at the winning fish. I guess it was so small he didn't see it.

He said, "What fish?" I told him to look again.

When he finally saw it he said, "You crazy or something? All mine were bigger than that one."

I asked him to prove it. "She throwed them back in the ocean."

"Mr. Michael, can you remember what I told you about not letting a kid beat me fishing and that I was going to find a way to beat him?"

"That was cheating!" he said.

"Yep!" But I started hoping he would catch a fish; if he didn't catch one, Bill and Doc were prepared to let everyone know Michael's fish were much bigger. He immediately started watching all four of the lines that were out. Soon, just as though we had planned it, a two- or three-pound fish was on the line and in the boat.

He looked at me and said, "Now, you see there? I told you that this lady would think I was a gentleman and the handsomest one, and help me catch the biggest one."

We made sure that he pulled the rest of the fish in. When we got back to the dock, he made Bill and Doc look at the two fish and tell me that his was the biggest. I told him I couldn't figure out how he did it.

He said, "I told you that I was going to whip you

and I'm going to tell all the kids at Winners Club too, and that I wasn't bragging; I whipped you. Didn't I?"

I told him, "I sure am happy that you didn't take me up on my $45 bet this morning. If you had, now I would be trying to figure out a way not to pay you. I'm glad you are not a gambling man."

After telling the captain goodbye and getting hugged about a dozen times by a truly beautiful and fantastic lady, we headed back to McDonald's for lunch.

Before going to the hotel, we stopped by the shopping center so we could relieve a fellow of burning pocket syndrome. He just had to get rid of the last of his money, that $45 that he had in one of his pockets.

He finally got to buy the plastic raft with paddle holes that he had seen the day before and needed desperately. That ate up $23 and some change—$22 bucks left. The Panama Jack T-shirt and cap he needed to wear to the beach and supper. Then he purchased a gift for each member of his family. All along I was warning him to be careful and not overdo it.

When I handed Mr. Michael six dollars at the checkout counter to clear up a situation that was about to become sticky, he smiled at me and winked. I winked back and said, "I won't tell."

He had to have help getting all his goodies into the car. Bill and the Doc sure were showing tons of patience. We were there shopping for quite a while.

It was 3 p.m. and we were back on the beach. While there he had several statements to make like "sun's real hot," "the water's cold," "everybody and his brother are on the beach," "I'm going to stay dry and not get my new Panama Jack T-shirt wet so I can wear it to supper," "the water's not clear—it's nasty looking," "hold my Panama Jack hat so it won't get wet," "see them sail boats—one turned over," "having fun," "my arms are getting red," "give me back my hat," and then came that famous statement, "watch me jump over them waves."

Well, "Panama Jack Gilreath" got slammed by a wave. He rushed out of the water, his new hat soaking wet and sitting sideways on his head and said, "Shoot! Can we get them dried before we go to supper?"

He was ready to go back to the room. I guess he was a little depressed about the Panama Jack accident. We put his shirt and hat on a chair out on the deck to dry, then back to the beach and on to the pier to watch a kite show.

While we were there, two young ladies in very revealing bathing suits strolled out of the crowd, each holding a beer can; one of those lovely ladies had a boom box on her shoulder and was dancing. In my opinion these two young ladies were not the prettiest girls on the beach. Michael looked at them for a moment while they danced, with the boom box music loud enough to get everybody's attention. But he noticed I had my eye on him.

He quickly looked away and I asked him "What is on your mind, my boy?"

He said very quietly, "I'm afraid this fishing dock might fall."

I said, "Bull! You were thinking and looking at those two pretty young ladies."

He looked at me and frowned. "Pretty? Are you blind and crazy?" I winked at him and he said, "You better not tell."

While Michael and I spent our evening on the beach, Bill and Doc went back to Captain Anderson's Restaurant planning the evening that Mr. Michael would never forget. We left the hotel at 7:30 p.m. for dinner, with Mr. Michael wearing his Panama Jack shirt and hat, that by then were dry.

As we walked into the room a magician stopped Michael and had him to assist him with several tricks that made Michael look great and me look like I couldn't count, see or feel, all with the audience's approval.

As we were led to our table by a beautiful lady, one of the entertainers (another beautiful lady) got Michael to come up on the stage while she sang "You

Light Up My Life," "I Will Always Love You," and "You Are My Best Friend."

I don't know if the audience knew about Michael or not, but while the lady led him back to our table everyone stood up and applauded. Then they brought a small cake to our table with a sparkler on top. We watched the sparkler go out and got a lot of applause again.

After our meal of fish and hushpuppies the people next to us were ordering martinis quite often, which Michael heard. About the same time they brought Michael some kind of giant ice cream float. He asked me what it was and I whispered to him that I thought it was called a "martuddi."

He just looked at me and smiled and said, "You're going crazy again. I don't believe it!" He was the center of attraction for about two hours, which was fantastic. Writing this is such a pleasure for me, because I'm getting to recall a happy time in a fantastic kid's life.

When we got back to our room, he called his mother and told her all that had happened. That short time was very emotional for the three adults who were standing there listening.

We all agreed later that it was an experience that will live with us until we die. We were told by Michael's mother later that she felt the same thing. That night Michael and I walked on the beach for a while, just having idle conversation, and went back to the room to pack our bags for the trip home the next morning.

When we settled into bed Michael said, "Boy, I had fun tonight! I'll make you a promise, Mr. Balliew."

"What's that, buddy?" I said.

"When I get to Heaven, I'm going to tell Jesus that I love you because you are nice to everybody and for Him to look out for you when you are fishing and stuff and everything."

"And I will make you a promise too, pal. When I say my prayers I'm going to ask Jesus to look out for you. And I'm going to ask him to send me a lot of kids just as nice as you to hang around with. Boy, it's been fun for me too! I know Mr. Bill and Mr. Doc feel the same way, too. See you in the morning pal!"

While lying there thinking about the day's events, I said the prayer I promised Michael I would say.

The next morning at 5:45 I realized Michael was already awake when I asked him if he would like to go to the beach real quick, just to walk. The waves were making that unforgettable sound and the moon was still in the sky.

As we walked I asked him what he was thinking about. He said, "It's pretty here and them birds are real fast runners and I have had the best time I ever had and I have the best buddy in the world!"

"You know I was thinking the same thing," I replied. I then asked him if he would like to take another refreshing frozen-brain shower and got that (by now) familiar answer, "Are you crazy or something!"

The flight home was uneventful. Michael slept most of the way without grabbing the safety harness a single time. We arrived in Calhoun about 1:30 p.m. on Sunday, May 7, 1982. There were several family members there to greet their now-famous fisherman.

The last sound on the tape I recorded was Bill and Doc telling Michael how much they enjoyed the time with him, along with a few comments I made before I gave Michael's mother a copy of the tape and pictures of Michael laughing and romping in the ocean.

I had the chance to see my pal several times in the following weeks, and each time I was around him I marveled at the courage and his spirit that was evident by the smile on his face. And each time we remembered to wink. Once when I didn't wink back as quickly as he thought I should have and he said with a wide smile, "You better not tell."

"About what? Those two lovely young ladies we saw on the dock," I said.

His last comment to me was, "Lovely young ladies! You are still crazy." He winked at me and I did the same, letting him know his secret was safe with me. I sure hope he will understand why I'm telling our secrets now.

The announcement in the newspaper stated, Mr. Mike Jurl Gilreath, 12, died at 10 a.m. Thursday, Aug. 26, 1982 in Gordon Hospital following a lengthy illness. The funeral was at 2 p.m. on the following Saturday at Plainview Baptist Church. The Winners Club members were honorary pallbearers and with three of his ocean-fishing buddies Bill Akins, Dr. Vern Dortch, and Deacon Balliew listed among the pallbearers.

I will always remember him and the things that he did for me and everyone else. I miss our close friendship, and the things he did to make me feel better about myself, and how he continues to make me smile.

70

Most of all I miss him. I know we will have a second chance to meet if I can remember the advice Mr. Michael gave me on several occasions. "You have to behave or you won't go to Heaven and be around Jesus and all them other fishermen and stuff."

The hundreds of times I have thought how bad I had it and started to worry, I many times considered what my little friend Michael told me: "Don't worry, cause I ain't."

If a kid could carry his kind of load and not worry, what in this world could be a heavier load than what he carried? I will always remember him as a lifelong friend; I know for sure he has kept his promise when he told me he would talk to Jesus and tell him he loved me and to look out for me and everything.

And I know that the Lord has answered my promise to Michael when I told him I would ask God and Jesus to send me a lot of kids just like him. I've had the chance to be around hundreds of special kids since those days over twenty-five years ago.

On Aug. 26, 2007, 27 years to the day my pal Michael died, a couple of friends and I stood in the Bethlehem Cemetery on Nottely Dam Road in Blairsville, in front of his grave—resting in a part of the country he liked so well and surrounded by relatives I had heard him talk about so many times.

Engraved on his tombstone is a kid with his feet in the water, sitting in the back of a flat-bottomed boat with fishing pole in his hand and a small dog by his side.

Anyone that sees it will know instantly the fellow had something to do with fishing. It was all to the left of his birth and death dates where a "dash" could have been placed.

"Well, buddy," I thought as I stood there, "all I planned to do with this story was to share a part of your life and to make sure a few people knew that yours was a very important dash to me. You only had a few years here with us and in everybody's opinion you made the best use of the time the Lord gave you."

I wondered again, as I have several times in the past, was one of his reasons for being here and around me to teach me? To teach me that no matter what my problems are someone has it worse and is coping with it like he did: "Don't worry, cause I ain't."

"I believe you had realized you were chosen by the best Fisherman of all times to be on His team. I know your fishing buddy, Jesus, is proud of you."

72

As I turned to leave I winked and could almost feel him saying, "You're gonna tell. I know you are but it's OK. I knew you couldn't keep it a secret anyway."

And I know I still got that wink.

The House Of Dreams

by Barry Giornelli
Staff writer for *The Calhoun Times*

One of Gordon County's most successful athletes is Jackie Proctor, who was a 16-year-old boy who attended the Liberty School for the Retarded in Gordon County when he first met the legendary Deacon Balliew. Proctor told Balliew he wanted to run races.

Like so many other children who have told Balliew their dreams, Proctor's dream came true in a "big-time" way. Armed with a stopwatch and a few training exercises Balliew got from a high school coach, Balliew and Proctor went to a track.

"We practiced real hard for two years," Balliew says.

Proctor entered local competitions and ran dashes that would have erased all the local high school records. Then, in 1979, he achieved the ultimate: he blazed a 200-meter race in the International Special Olympics in Brockport, N.Y. in 22 seconds, flat.

A picture of Proctor wearing the gold medal he won that day hangs on the wall of a house on Sugar

Valley Road called "The Winners Club," a unique organization founded by Balliew, who is a juvenile court probation officer.

The Winners Club has become a house of dreams for hundreds of Gordon County children.

Here, Deacon Balliew and his volunteers are taking children who seem destined for troubled, unhappy lives and turning them into "winners."

Mike, a mentally handicapped young man, told Balliew his dream was to go hunting. Balliew recalls the day Mike downed a deer with a bow and arrow.

"We were walking the road and I saw the deer," Balliew says. "Mike saw him too, and as the deer walked from the woods onto the road, I saw Mike pull his bow back. I saw the flight of the arrow. It hit the mark, and Mike's dream came true."

Tony had a dream to go deep sea fishing someday. That dream came true, too. Balliew took Tony and six or eight of the Winners Club Boy Scouts to Florida and chartered a boat for a deep-sea expedition in the Gulf of Mexico.

The wall on which Proctor's gold medal hangs holds a collage of mementos of other children's achievements: Boy Scout awards by the dozens;

76

ribbons for Cherokee Capital Fairs; photographs of "disadvantaged" children doing what most adults only dream of.

Winners Club members doing things like going to Braves games, trips to Washington, D.C., bowling, rebuilding car engines....

The club defies definition. There are disabled children in it, but it's not for the disabled. There are kids with disciplinary problems, but it's not just for them, either.

Rebecca Owen, director of the Gordon County Untied Way, describes them as children who are disadvantaged because of their social upbringing, home environment, or mental or physical disabilities.

"These kids for the most part don't have a say-so in what was handed to them. They just had to swallow what the world has dished out," she says

"Deacon just looks for the best in them tries to see what they are good at and what they would succeed in, if given a chance... Even if it's just a glimmer, he zeroes in on something the child can do. He gives them their pride back, and that's not something easily done."

Balliew says the secret to Winners Club is "L-O-

V-E. You'll feel it when you come in here. You can't leave this place without feeling it."

It's hard to believe something that simple can do so much—unless you visit the Winners Club and see Balliew and the children interact.

The clubhouse has a downstairs area where high school students are busy tutoring children. Balliew, meanwhile is talking to a young girl he calls "Blondie."

"How many times have I told you you're beautiful?" Balliew asks.

"A hundred," Blondie says.

"How many times have I told you you're big-time nice?"

"About six hundred."

"All you've got to do," Balliew says, "is do around other people the way you do around me. Why do you think I love you so much, because you're mean as a striped snake?"

Blondie shakes her head and giggles.

"Because you're big-time nice?"

She laughs and nods.

"Kids don't make many mistakes," Balliew says later. "Adults make mistakes, and children learn from adults," he says. "How hard is it to tell a kid he's perfect, because he is? He's made in God's image."

That approach has helped Balliew help kids since 1968, when he took three Calhoun boys on a hotdog roast. From there, he stared a Boy Scout troop, and asked each of the scouts what their dreams were. One by one, he made those dreams reality.

The Boy Scout troop evolved into something bigger—the Winners Club—and it has since gained national and international attention.

And all this had been done without dues of any type or a penny of taxpayer money. The $100,000 clubhouse, for instance, was built from private contributions and the labor of some of the club's founders.

A visitor can hardly take a step in or around the house without encountering evidence of little folks' accomplishments:

Outside, there is a garden maintained by Winners Club Girl Scouts, led by Balliew's wife, Inez. The garden wouldn't have been possible if it weren't for a crew of boys, who dug a series of trenches to drain the once swampy area where the garden now stands. Inside the house are hundreds of jars of home-grown vegetables the Girls Scouts have canned.

Take a walk into the kitchen and you're liable to feel taller than usual: the counters are lower than waist-high for most adults, but they're perfect for a child who's helping to cook or wash dishes.

Now go to the bedroom and you'll see an antique chest of drawers. It was rescued from a landfill, repaired, and refinished beautifully by the oldest club members as a summer project—their own idea, Balliew says.

A pair of leg braces lies on a shelf in another room. They were once worn by a disabled child whose doctor said he would probably never walk without them.

In the hallway there is a display case containing hundreds of arrowheads—all found by club members.

Another display case holds Civil War minie balls they found at the Resaca battle site with a metal detector.

United Way donations keep the program going, Balliew says. So do church donations, such as clothing in the winter. Individuals donate. The tutors are volunteers: high school Honor Society students, the Fellowship of Christian Athletes, school counselors, and teachers all give their after-hours time to help.

"This community needs to know how they've changed people's lives," Balliew says. "I want them to understand that all this financial help and all the volunteer hours have made the world a better place for many of our troubled children."

George Caron, chairman of the Winners Club board of directors, agrees that the club is a community accomplishment.

"For all the years the Winners Club has been in existence, this community has supported it," Caron says. "We have zealously rejected offers of public funds—state, county and federal—because of the strings attached. We don't take any strings-attached funds.

And although many volunteers help Balliew, Caron says they "have always chosen to be low profile.

81

People don't stand in line to take credit for what's done. No one has ever received a red cent in compensation."

And the community effort has resulted in tangible benefits for the community, according to Owen and others.

Children that seemed to be heading for the court system—and contributing to court costs paid by the public—are out on successful, productive courses, Owen says. (Many of the club's first members are now attending college or have already found white-collar jobs.) More words of high praise come from Lane Bearden, Gordon County's juvenile court judge.

The Winners Club has all but eliminated a sad problem that other county's juvenile courts are seeing, Bearden says: mentally disabled children getting into trouble with the law.

"Surrounding counties have all had difficulties with special needs children who have juvenile court problems," Bearden says. "But we have almost no cases of that sort because of the Winners Club."

Yellow Dandelions and Kids

by Inez "Mama" Balliew

When you and I look at a patch of dandelions, we see a bunch of weeds that are going to take over our yard. Our kids see flowers for somebody and blowing white stuff you can make a wish on.

When we look at an old beggar and he smiles at us we see a smelly, dirty person who probably wants money and we look away. Our kids see someone smiling at them and they smile back.

When we hear music we love, we know we can't carry a tune and don't have much rhythm so we sit self-consciously and listen. Our kids feel the beat and move to it. They sing out the words. If they don't know them, they make up their own.

When we feel wind on our face, we brace ourselves against it. We feel it messing up our hair and pushing us back when we walk. Our kids close their eyes, spread their arms and fly with it, until they fall to the ground laughing.

When we pray, we say "thee" and "thou" and "grant me this, give me that." Our kids say, "Hi God!

85

Thanks for my toys and my friends. Please keep the bad dreams away tonight. Sorry, I don't want to go to Heaven yet. I would miss my Mommy and Daddy and friends."

When we see a mud puddle we step around it. We see muddy shoes and dirty carpets. Our kids sit in it. They see dams to build, rivers to cross, and worms to play with.

I wonder if we are given kids to teach or to learn from. No wonder God loves the little children!

Enjoy the little things in life, for one day you may look back and realize they were the big things.

Beautiful Blue-eyed Kids

It was only a few days before Christmas. As usual, the Spirit of the season had not caught up with me, even though shoppers' cars packed the parking area of our local K-Mart discount store.

Inside the store, it was worse. Shopping carts and last minute shoppers jammed the aisles. I looked around and said, "Lord why do I have to be doing this?" I had a slight headache, and heartburn I could have prevented by not eating that super-hot chili at lunch, and the finger I sprained putting a bicycle together I had just hit on the buggy handle, so it was sending pains all the way to my shoulder.

I had a list that I painstakingly put together. It contained the "wants" of the people who told me I didn't have to buy them anything, but would let me know by their look that their feelings were hurt if I didn't buy them something. "What a chore," I thought. I was buying for somebody that has everything under the sun, and knew I was going to frown at the cashier and whistle my displeasure at the cost when she totaled my purchase. I guess you can say I was not a happy camper, and for certain I was not having fun. Thinking back, I must have been reacting like that fellow Mr. Scrooge that we have all heard about.

I rushed up and down the aisles getting bumped by those speeding, impolite, blind, last-minute shopping cart pushers. After getting the last unwanted gift I headed for that dreadful check out line. I walked back and forth looking for the shortest line. Even after I found it, it still meant a 30-minute wait.

I decided to walk around for a while; I didn't feel like waiting in line so long and with a few minutes walking around the lines just might become shorter. As I walked I started watching little kids' faces as they looked at all the bright lights and pretty toys. Each kid had wide-open eyes that sparkled; I guess that's the best way to describe the eyes I was seeing.

In the toy aisle I noticed a little four- or five-year-old boy with a ragged coat and too-large shoes that made a flapping sound when he jumped up and down in his excitement. He held to his mother's shopping cart with a firm grip, and in her cart were two little red-headed toddlers; at a glance you knew they were brothers or sisters that could have passed as twins. They even had matching catsup stains on their wrinkled clothes.

As I looked closer at them I did what I always have done: I began to focus on their eyes. "Clear-as-crystal blue" and "beautiful" are exactly the words to describe their eyes, and the eyes showed the little ones' excitement. I continued to follow and listen to their discussions with their mother. I have lost most of my hearing over the years, so most times I try to look at people's faces and that helps me to know what's going on.

I didn't need to see those little fellows' faces. I could hear very well as they asked their mother if Santa Claus could bring them every toy in sight. I remember thinking that a child is wonderful no matter what economic or social situation they come from. After a few minutes observing, I couldn't stand it any longer—I had to say something to the three about Santa Claus.

"You guys know it won't be long before Santa comes to see all the kids around here," I said. For the first time I really looked at the mother. She had dark circles under her eyes and a face full of depression and sadness, but did manage a smile when I said to her, "I hope all three of your kids have been sweet so Santa will come to see them."

I thought as I started to walk away their mother looked familiar and before I had a chance to say anything she asked, "Are you Deacon Balliew?"

"I sure am," I said.

"I remember you; when I was a little kid you came to our house a lot and was a friend of my mother's," she said.

"When was that?"

"When you was a juvenile officer and you had come to take my brother to the Court House. I remember hearing that he might be sent to the YDC because he had been acting pretty bad. My mother was holding me when you reached over and hugged my neck and told me not to be afraid or worry; you would take good care of him."

90

"What is your name?" I asked. When she told me it was like bells ringing; it brought back memories of wonderful Christmases long ago.

I had been blessed for the past three decades with the chance to provide, along with a group of friends, Christmas gifts to kids and their families that needed help. We always insisted that the parents not tell their families and especially their children that we had helped. Santa Claus always brought the gifts. Christmas and its meaning was always there when the parents came to pick up or we delivered the gifts.

There were many hugs, tears and thanks from parents who could not afford to ask Santa Claus to bring very much. Especially the food. When I think of the food and little fellows eating on Christmas day, it gets to me every time. I knew they always needed it. I have very fond memories of seeing hams or turkeys sitting on tables waiting for the Christmas dinner.

I asked her if she remembered when I talked to her mother several times about Santa. "Yes, I can remember that, and especially you talking to me when I was just a little girl. My mother is dead now," she said.

"I know. I saw it in the paper and I'm sorry," I told her.

"My mother loved you to death," she said. "And that surprised everybody, because you were a law officer... especially all my aunts, uncles and cousins, who most had been in, or were, in jail. She told me later that you had helped with our Christmas several times. My Daddy never did help my Mama much; all he would do was drink all the time. He is dead now, too. I sure do miss my Mama a lot, especially now. She died right after Christmas three year ago."

I suddenly realized we were holding up speedier shoppers; I had been hit on the leg once and knew we had better move. I asked the little fellow to help push my shopping cart while I talked to his mother. Before we stopped in the center of store I knew I had made a mistake; that little guy almost broke my ankle, foot and leg before I realized I had better do the steering for him.

When I asked her how she was doing she said, "Well, you knew my first husband; he got killed in that wreck four years ago. Do you remember the boy who lived close to us, the boy who was with my brother when he got in trouble?"

I told her I did but thought he got sent to prison for years.

"He did" she said "But he got out three years ago and I married him and we were doing pretty good, I guess, until the other day when they arrested him for selling and smoking dope. He's got about six more years of probation and will probably be going back to prison again. I don't know what I'm going to do."

"What about your family?"

"I don't have no family here. All of them are dead or in jail or live somewhere else; I'm by myself and don't know what I'm going to do," she said.

I looked down at the little guy with the wrinkled coat and matted hair that had a good hold on my buggy. I told him, "Little buddy, do you know that I know Santa Claus? He is my good friend; he is such a good friend he lets me call him Sam Claus. He really is my buddy."

With those crystal-clear bright blue eyes staring at me he asked, "You really know Santa Claus?"

"Yep, I know him pretty good and will be talking to him in a couple of days."

"You will... you will really see him and talk to Santa Claus some time?" he asked. I looked up at his mother and saw tears welling up in her eyes.

She started to say something when I interrupted

her. "Yes, lady, I sure do know Santa Claus—you know I do. You have known that since you was a little girl haven't you?"

She said she did and with her acknowledging what I was saying he knew I had to be telling the truth.

I continued, "And I am going to tell him just exactly what you tell me these three guys want for Christmas. And maybe he will stop on your roof and sneak into your house with a bunch of toys and goodies." I looked at the two little fellows in the cart who were all eyes; the two year old was taking in every word and staring at me, trying to figure out this stranger who had her mother showing those kinds of emotions.

I touched her on the hand and said, "Yes beautiful, I am going to see Santa and I'm going to tell him I know the prettiest girl in the world that has blond hair and has been a super sweet kid, too."

The little boy turned loose of my cart with the gifts I'd had such a struggle choosing and said, "Are you going to tell him about her too?" as he pointed to his little sister.

"Are you kidding? I'm telling him about her first because she is so sweet."

94

"She ain't sweet all the time; some times she pitches fits and Mama has to give her a whuppin'."

I told the little sister, "You better be sweet or Santa Claus won't come to see you." I then warned my little buddy, "You don't need to say that kind of stuff too loud because Santa Claus could be peeping around the corner and could hear what you are saying."

His mother said, "See there, I told you—he is everywhere." To me she said, "Deacon Balliew, you don't have to do this." I could see and feel her pride, but her *love* for her three overshadowed that pride. Boy, did that mother ever read my mind in a hurry. Or maybe she remembered her youth and how a group had helped her mother when there was such a need in her family. She told me, "I have been telling them about Santa Claus and Christmas for a while. Hearing you telling them about Santa Claus... it's just like I've been telling them."

After I found out where she lived and made arrangements to see them the next day, I put a few dollars in her hand for whatever she might need. I saw that she began to get tears in her eyes again, but interrupted when I said. "Boy, you fellows really live way out in the country. I'll have to tell Santa where you

95

live when I see him."

The mother said, " I'm so proud we saw you; you are the only one besides me who has told them this year about Santa Claus. It sure sounds better coming from someone else, and I can tell they believe every word you told them. I believe she understands, too," and she pointed to the baby.

I knew exactly where they lived and it really was out in the country. I also knew some of her not-so-law-abiding neighbors. As I started to leave the mother said, "Deacon Balliew I can't believe this; I was worried to death. I didn't know what I was going to do. You're something, you know that?" She hugged my neck but most gratifying was when that little girl also reached to give me a hug. And of course by now I had a little buddy who reached up and gave me the third hug I had gotten in seconds.

I leaned over and gave the baby a quick hug and told them, "I'll see you fellows tomorrow and talk about Santa Claus some more."

The mother said, "Thank you, Deacon Balliew. You better watch out for the mud hole on the right side of the drive way—it is really deep. A log truck got stuck and made a deep hole; their daddy was going to fill it up but didn't seem to ever get time to do it."

I told her I would, that I had to go and would see them tomorrow, then turned away and headed for the dreaded checkout.

Suddenly I realized the checkout line didn't seem so bad after all. And that's even though the lines were longer than when I was in my bad heartburn, headache, sore sprained finger mood. While I was in line I saw my new friends and their mother leaving the store without buying anything. I saw them waving good by to me, even the baby waved. I said the prayer I have said many times in the past. I guess I pray a little different than most people. I think a prayer with my eyes open. "Thank you Lord. You know I'm going to need a lot of help with this situation I've got myself in. Amen."

When the lady finished totaling my purchase of gifts for people whose feelings would be hurt if I hadn't bought them something, I didn't frown or whistle at the cost. And I didn't feel like being grouchy or acting like Mr. Scrooge about those last-minute gifts. The people whose feelings I hadn't cared about while shopping a few minutes ago seemed to have taken on a different meaning now. Even the catsup stains on my shirt two babies put there while giving me a hug didn't look all that bad; matter of fact, they looked pretty nice, since I knew who put them there.

On the way home I started thinking, "Man, my feelings changed fast." I knew exactly why: three little kids with wrinkled clothes and uncombed dirty hair, but with bright sparkling eyes and catsup on their faces—that's why. A caring mother, whom I knew without a doubt needed help. And of course, the Lord had reminded me again that he gave us his son Jesus. I knew the Christmas spirit I didn't have an hour ago was surely there now, and I knew I had work to do. I had already spent all the funds donated for other kids and their families.

The next morning I got on the phone to my three friends (J.W.H., C.H. and T.B.) who always told me if I needed anything to let them know. I got a commitment to help and was on my way to my new buddies' house. As I turned into the long driveway, I was surprised to see a hunter standing by his truck. It was stuck in the mud hole the kids' mother told me about. Deep was not the word to describe what I was looking at; maybe a bottomless pit was a better word.

I took the hunter for help and returned to the family's trailer. My little buddy was waiting at the door with those bright eyes and smile. His first words were, "Did you see him?"

"See who?" I asked.

"Santa Claus, the real Santa Claus," he said.

"Nope, but I hope to see him soon; I have to know what to tell him you and your sisters want him to bring you for Christmas," I replied.

I thought, "This little guy sure acts older than his four or five years." I looked for the girls, who were not in sight, and asked the mother where they were.

She said, "Those two sleep late every day. But this young man I could not get in bed until 11 o'clock and he was up at daylight. When I asked him why he was up so early he said he was looking for Santa Claus. Boy, he sure is excited about Santa! Last night at K-mart you made a friend. He talked about 'that man who talks to Santa Claus' non-stop.

"Deacon Balliew, a Sheriffs detective followed me home last night and asked me about several men, and wanted to know if I knew them and did my husband have any friends that visited here very often. This has me worried. What is he trying to do? I didn't even know he was selling marijuana or other drugs. I knew he smoked that stuff, I could tell because he got

99

mad a lot when he was. I wish I didn't live away out here."

Why don't you move?" I asked her.

"I don't have money to move, and I looked at our heating gas tank gauge this morning and it shows about empty."

"Do you think your husband has any money at the jail? If he has I'll get it for you. Was he working before he got locked up?"

"He said he had a job, but I didn't believe him," she said. "He never had money like he had a job."

"You told me last night you didn't have any relatives around. Is that the truth?"

"I have an aunt in Dalton and a sister in Alabama."

"Can either one help you in any way to get out of this mess you are in?" I asked.

"I don't know how to get hold of them. I don't think they would help anyway," was her reply.

"Have you been in contact with your husband since he has been in jail?"

"I went to see him last Sunday and he told me his probation officer had told him he wouldn't be going to court until after Christmas; he told me he thinks he will be out before then. I'm supposed to go see him Sunday but don't know how I will get there. If you hadn't loaned me that money last night I would be out of food right now. And sure would not have enough gas to go back and forth to the jail."

I looked at her. "If you are that broke, what in the world were you doing at K mart last night?"

"I had got worried," she replied. "It's only a week until Christmas and we had only been to town one time this month. I had been telling them about Christmas and Santa Claus. And the kids really needed to go see all the Christmas lights and toys. I knew I had enough gas to get there and back so I went."

I had spent several years working with people that would take advantage of a person in a flash or without a second thought, and was sort of skeptical of this mother's story. So I decided to see if I could find out if she was being completely truthful with me. I went to the Sheriffs Department, to see what her husband's charges were and to talk to him.

I realized I had been in their house about 30 minutes and my little buddy had not said a word. I asked him, "Why are you so quiet, little pal?"

His answer really caught me off guard. "I'm

scared about Mama being afraid when she cried last night all time. I help mama all time, don't I mama? I'm a big boy, ain't I mama?"

Before his mother said a word I told him how proud I was that we had become buddies because a fellow needs all the friends he can get, and that I planned to come back to see them. I also said I hoped his sisters were awake when I got back this afternoon, and I thought I would be able to see Santa in town and when I did, I would tell him where they lived.

Right then the serious thinking was gone and I saw those bright blue eyes light up. He was staring at me and had this infectious smile. I wondered, "What has this little fellow has been through? What has he seen in his young life?" I handed the mother some money and told her to get food and whatever they needed and that I would be back that afternoon.

As I left their home I thought my prayer again, "Please Lord, help me with this situation I've gotten myself in. Amen." That family sounded genuine and I knew I was going to help, but how much help was going to be needed? And was I being too suspicious? Those kids were important and I needed to be thinking of them.

102

As I went toward the jail in Calhoun I thought about what I had seen: no Christmas tree, no decorations, a filthy house, no food, a little boy acting older than his years and trying to protect his mother... a family who was destitute, and most importantly, a mother I was beginning to believe was telling me the truth. No matter if she was honest with me or not, I still had work to do. I could not get those crystal-clear, bright blue eyes out of my mind.

When I arrived at the Sheriff's Department I met with the investigator in charge of the father's case. I was shocked to find out that his charges in this county were nothing compared to the charges against him in another county. I asked the detective if he were found guilty of the charges, what would happen to him.

He told me that warrants were being taken as we were speaking, and if found guilty he would be serving at least 10 years. He was to be transferred to the other county sometime later that day.

I went into the jail's visiting area and met with the father. I asked him if he knew his wife didn't have money to buy food or Christmas gifts for the children. I also asked if he had any money tucked away to share with them and if he had any relatives that could help them until he got out of jail.

He said, "Mr. Balliew, you know, I lived with my grandmother; we never heard from my parents or knew where they were, and still don't know. I don't have any money. I think I will be getting out of jail in a couple of days and I will take care of my family myself."

I told him I knew his family would be happy to see him at home.

"How do you know about my family?" he asked. "And how are they doing? Are they OK?"

I told him, "I saw them last night at K-Mart, Christmas shopping."

"Then why are you asking if I have any money? She must have been spending the money I left with her."

"I just thought they might need a few dollars to help them out." I told him I would see him later. I knew it would be much later, if ever. From what I saw and heard, those kids would be better off that Christmas without their father around.

I thought several of those "Mr. Scrooge" thoughts again as I walked out of there. One of them was, "Why in the world does this man have the responsibility of raising little kids?"

I left the jail knowing I was going to need lots of help, and headed home to get the best judge of females I have ever known: my wife Inez Balliew (now deceased.) I knew if she could meet the mother, she could determine in a few seconds if the lady was serious and if we would be able to help.

I found her at home; I had already told her about meeting the mother and her three kids the previous night. After telling her about everything that had happened that day, we were on our way to the country to visit the family. As we pulled into their yard, out the door came the little guy to meet us.

"Who is she?" he asked.

"My boy," I told him, "she is the lady who tells Santa Claus about kids who need something for Christmas."

He dashed inside, yelling, "My buddy is back with a Santa Claus lady." I introduced the mother to Inez and asked for the two oldest kids to come outside with me while the Santa Lady talked to their mother.

I was surprised how fast the little girl came to me. Maybe I was making some inroads with her. While we were outside I saw the skinniest dog I have ever seen. He wasn't skinny for the lack of food—he was

105

just plain skinny. I couldn't tell what breed he was, probably an all-American.

"What is his name, and will your dog bite me?" I asked the kids.

"His name is Doggy. Nope, he won't bite, and he can't bark none, neither," I was told.

"Why?" I asked.

"A car run over him and broke his barking hickey." My pal said that like an expert on dog barking hickeys. While walking around I noticed wet clothes on a clothes line and asked my expert pal how they got there and was informed that his Mother had washed them in the bathtub and hung them up there.

"They sure look nice and clean to me," I told him.

"Yep," he said.

I thought how lucky I was to have a precious little red-haired two-year-old girl in my arms and my little pal feeling comfortable around me. I thought another prayer, "Thank you, Lord, for your help with this situation I got myself into."

I noticed Inez and the mother standing at the door of the trailer. As I approached she said, "Let the two kids come inside for a minute so we can talk."

106

Once outside her first words were, "We have got to help this girl and her babies; they are in trouble. I told the mother to pack their clothes and we would be back to get them in a little while."

We headed to our car, waving at the kids; I was surprised to see how quickly the two oldest waved back. I told my little buddy I would see him later. His reply was, "I will see you in a little while, buddy."

In the car I turned to Inez. "Man that was quick! What did she say to get your attention that fast?"

"She didn't say that much. Can you believe those kids didn't have a Christmas last year? She told me the father said they were too young to know about a Christmas or Christmas tree. I believe she was telling the truth. I didn't see a Christmas tree or any sign of Christmas decorations this time, either.

"I saw some baby formula and bottles, three cans of spaghetti and meatballs, a couple packs of oatmeal, a box of cereal, a pack of crackers and some Kool Aid. The stove is broken, so they only have a hot plate to cook on. The fridge doesn't work; the clothes washer is broken and so is the commode seat.

"There's a mattress on the bedroom floor they all sleep on; the house smelled awful, roaches every where, not many dishes or pots and pans, only a couple sets of clothes for each kid, no hope of buying any either. That girl is very depressed, but I can tell she loves her babies to death.

"We will have to find them a place to live; you can go by and see her landlord—you know him very well—and see how they stand."

The only response I had after I spent a second trying to think about all she had said was, "Wonder where she and those babies can spend the Christmas holidays?"

She told me, "She and those babies can stay at the house during Christmas holidays while you get things worked out for her."

"I get things worked out for her?" was the only response I had time to make.

"The downstairs has already been decorated for kids and those babies will have a warm, clean place for Santa to come and visit."

I knew I had to say OK, or I would hear those threats of being called Mr. HumBug Scrooge. Those threats were getting on my nerves; was I really acting like Mr. Scrooge or were they joking? I was afraid to ask.

I didn't tell her how wonderful I thought it would be to have little ones in the house to help make this a Christmas they would always remember: making their wait for Santa to arrive a lot of fun for everyone, especially me, and letting them know they were wonderful kids that were loved. I know there was one old geezer who was getting attached to a little guy he called his Buddy and a sandy-red blonde little girl, both with bright blue eyes.

When we arrived home Inez said, "You can go see her landlord, while I get every thing ready for them and to make sure every thing is baby-proof." That word "baby-proof" hadn't been used around our house in several years and it sounded great.

I was getting into the Christmas spirit again big time, thinking about telling Christmas stories I knew our three had never heard. I could see my little pal and his sister in my lap listening to the story about Baby Jesus. I thought about them never having a Christmas, and I almost didn't like the father. But with the Christmas Spirit and all that Mr. Scrooge stuff I didn't want to think about anything negative, just Santa Claus.

I went by their landlord's and got more bad news. The family was months behind with their rent, he also told me he had been paying the electricity and letting them stay there because of he kids. He asked if had I seen those cute kids. When I told him their story, he told me to get back with him after the holidays. With paying him out of the immediate picture I would be better able to help.

I arrived back at the house and found Mrs. Balliew irritated because I had taken too much time. We were on our way to get our Christmas guests and I was excited; trying to not let it show was a tough job.

We arrived at the trailer and found all of them packed and ready. Mrs. Balliew rode with the mother and the babies, while my pal rode with me. Away we went to the Balliew's house. I have to tell you: my little pal was nothing but constant sound; he never quit talking. The questions came so fast I finally told him that he would have to wait and ask Santa Claus all those questions because I didn't know the answers.

"You are Santa Claus's buddy," he stated. "Why don't you know?"

I just kept quiet. I knew I was in trouble. I had an expert riding with me and if I didn't have the right answer I would have a dozen more questions. Before we got home I thought, "How can a fellow as small as
110

this guy have so much lung power?"

I had to control my urge to think about being Mr. Scrooge. I saw the mother through my rear view mirror and knew she was crying because she was wiping away tears.

We finally got home with our precious cargo; all went down stairs except yours truly. I needed a few minutes of peace and quiet to rekindle my faculties. I thought, "That little guy did not have anybody to talk with and be a friend, except his mother." I went downstairs in a few minutes and heard the little girl talking nonstop like her brother had. Both were talking about the Christmas tree, the lights, Santa Claus, angels and candy. I had a chance to ask the mother why they didn't have a tree at home.

She said, "We didn't have one or any lights. He said he was going to buy some but he got put in jail before he could. I wanted to get some but I didn't have any money."

I asked her, "Where did you get money for gas for the car and food?"

She told me, "When they came and arrested him they made him leave all his stuff at the house. He had eight dollars and 35 cents, and that was all. I used it to

111

go to town and that is when we saw you and I bought a few groceries with it and the money you gave me."

Our two small guests were all eyes and questions. I knew they had never seen a home that was ready for Santa Claus to leave toys.

"How does Santa Claus get in your house? Mama said he walks into our house," my pal asked.

"He comes through our front door sneaky and quiet, leaves all the toys and other goodies under the tree and then sneaks out without making the first sound," I told him as convincingly as I could. It must have worked; he wanted to go upstairs to see where Santa Claus would sneak in.

I told Inez I was going to check with out local Children's Services and a few other agencies about help for our newfound family after Christmas. As I started to leave, Inez asked me to come back downstairs for a second and explain who I was going to see about help. Inez had tried to explain to the mother that the Family and Children Services were not going to take her kids because they were deprived or without a proper parent to take care of them, when they were in our house.

The mother said she had been warned by the police officers that arrested her husband about her house and stuff. I told her not to worry, as I was only going to see them about helping and talk to the other agencies about help in finding a place for all of them to live after Christmas. I assured her that I would look out for her and the kids.

I saw representatives of all the agencies and was assured that they would help the family after Christmas. It must have been the Christmas spirit.

On the way back home it hit me again: how did this all happen in one evening and a day? I knew it had to be the Lord's work; everything seemed to fall into place too well. Again I thought a prayer, "Lord, thanks for helping us with this situation I got myself in. Thank you for your guidance and the love I feel. I know you care about those little fellows, and Lord, help that mother to know and understand that we care, and with your help every thing is going to be okay. I know you can feel the love she has for those kids better than I can and all that love comes from you. Thank you Lord for the love you had for us when you gave your son Jesus during this Christmas season. Amen."

When I got home it was suppertime and everyone was at the table in a fantastic mood. The little girl was singing "Rudolph the Red-nosed Reindeer"

113

and was encouraged to sing it for me. When I heard her sing, "Red roof deer coming to town," I told her she made me real happy and I loved her. Of course, then my little buddy had to sing it for me, too—with about as much success. Inez had the baby in her lap and I was informed she was working on her second serving of potatoes.

What I saw was a little family getting comfortable with their surroundings and about to have a Christmas they would never forget. I asked them, "Do you want to go to K- Mart in a little while and look for what you want Santa Claus to bring you for Christmas?" That got everyone's attention.

"We have to write him a letter tomorrow evening. We'll put in the wood heater so it will burn and make a bunch of smoke that the wind will blow all the way to the North Pole, where Santa Claus and his reindeer live. Santa will use his magic to read that smoke, and just maybe he will bring you what you wrote in your letter." I got a couple of wonderful puzzled looks.

"So look close at the toys when you get to K-Mart so I can help you write the letter." You talk about little ones paying attention—we had them.

I looked at the kids' mother and noticed she didn't have the circles under her eyes and her face didn't look as swollen. She was really smiling and said, "How will I ever repay you and Mrs. Balliew for what you are doing? I can't believe these kids like you so much. They usually run and hide when someone comes to our house. I sure hope they don't break anything downstairs."

Mrs. Balliew took care of that by telling her we knew what was down stairs and there was nothing to worry about.

Our guest went downstairs. I stayed upstairs to explain to Spunkie, our boy and the best friend I've ever had in my life, about what was happening. Spunkie is a creature of habit and when his routine is interrupted he gets very quiet, confused and edgy. When I explained that all the kids downstairs would be writing a letter to Santa Claus when he did, Spunkie seemed to settle down. Santa Claus is, and always has been, important in his life.

As we drove into K-Mart's parking lot, to everyone's surprise Santa Claus was there. He was sitting on his makeshift throne on the sidewalk and doing his happy "Ho-ho-ho" laugh, greeting shoppers

115

as they entered the store. I will always remember my little buddy's loss of bravery when we got close to the season's favorite man. He grabbed hold of my hand and ducked behind me as we approached Santa.

Santa Claus must have been the real thing; he got very quiet as our three checked him out for a few seconds. I didn't help very much. My brave buddy only stared at him and wouldn't speak; I told him that this was Santa and he could talk to him. He told me we would write him a letter and he dashed by on his way inside the store. The little girl turned her head and wouldn't look at all.

The aisles were horribly jammed and I noticed the checkout lines snaked back into the store. I had that Scrooge feeling creeping over me again. "Man, how will I be able to tolerate that checkout line? I'll just have to grit my teeth and bear it."

Have you ever tried to kill a couple of hours in a jam-packed discount department store during the Christmas rush? If you haven't, you need to subject yourself to a little bit of it. I had decided that Spunkie and I would let the ladies and kids do the Christmas shopping; I knew I would get big-time nervous at such a slow pace.

On several occasions I passed our excited shoppers and could hear them asking for every toy on the shelves. I also noticed a shopping cart loaded with clothes. I spotted a little pink dress that was absolutely beautiful, and couldn't wait to see that precious little girl in it.

I spotted our crew a few minutes later with an empty shopping cart and found that Mrs. Balliew had asked a friend in layaway to hold them until I could pick them up. Boy, was I glad about that! I knew I could get the lady to check out all they had purchased in layaway. No check out lines! I sure did love those two ladies for sparing me grief.

After we got home, I went downstairs to see my newfound little buddies in bed. How precious they were! Their mother said they were very tired and went to sleep almost immediately after their baths. Inez was standing there and said, "How on this earth could a person deprive a child of Christmas? I will never understand. Look at their faces." I looked and noticed how the blinking Christmas tree lights made their now-clean hair sparkle.

I thought, "I am a lucky man. How many people in their lives get to see and feel what we are seeing and feeling at this moment?" Thank the Lord we had the chance to see his work being done. In one evening and a day all this had happened. I could hardly wait until the next day. And we had two more days before Santa would come to our house.

The Christmas Spirit. How could you not have it? I knew one other thing for sure: no more Mr. Scrooge at my house. Maybe a little bit of Mr. Scrooge at K-Mart in the checkout line…

Before I went to bed I prayed. "Lord, thank you for sharing your love with both our families and showing us how important it is for us to remember what you said about suffering the little children to come to you. I know Lord, now especially, what you meant by that. Please Lord, help me to be humble enough to always see children's needs. Amen."

The next two days were not nearly as eventful as the first two. When we went back to the kids' home to get some of the mother's belongings, my little buddy said, "You go, Mama. I'll stay in the car."

"Why don't you come and help Mama?" the mother asked. I looked at the little fellow and he was shaking his head "no." I could understand why; he must have had pretty bad memories of that place. Now he was developing memories he didn't want to lose.

The other interesting time was explaining to my little buddy the process of writing a letter to Santa Claus: how we would put in the heater so it would burn and make smoke, then Santa Claus could use his magic to read it so he would know what gifts they wanted. On that list were: a tricycle, fire truck, a pretty coat and some candy.

Every thing was going smoothly until my mister-know-it-all buddy got too close to the heater door, inhaled a lung full of the magic readable smoke and almost got choked. I asked him when he finished coughing and sputtering how he liked the Santa Claus letter business. He informed me that he had smelled smoke one time when his Daddy set the woods afire and it made him cough and his nose and eyes burn that time, too.

I guess having the three little fellows in our home on such short notice was the biggest event of all. To be honest, I was having the time of my life. I can truthfully say all the adults in our home were having one of the best Christmases ever.

I had picked up all the toys and clothes, and the prettiest pink dress I had ever seen in my life the day before and had left them with a friend to be picked up on Christmas Eve.

It was now Christmas Eve. Our family and our wonderful guests had spent a couple of hours seeing our community's Christmas lights and that had those bright blue eyes shining. I had the kids' mother sitting behind me, sniffling a lot.

She leaned over and said, "I have never seen my kids this happy in their lives. And the baby has smiled and laughed more lately than any time in her life. She will not come to me as long as Mrs. Balliew has her."

I thought about how sad it was for a mother to be caught in a situation like hers, not knowing how to get herself and her children out. When she told me at K-Mart a few nights before that she didn't know what she was going to do... well, I understood that a lot better now. I now knew she and her children were trapped in an abusive situation, by a father who was on drugs and didn't care about his family or anything else.

I know one day that man would wake up and realize he had the best family he could have asked for, and they will be gone. I knew one thing: if that mother wanted me to help them start a new beginning I would do it in a heartbeat.

120

Back at home, it was time for baths and pajamas. That baby was absolutely beautiful in her new pajamas with kittens on the front. When she and the other two smiled at me, I have to admit I was wrapped around all three kids' little fingers.

I've experienced many things and times with children in my life. I have to tell you, when I had those two little girls sitting on my lap staring at me with those crystal-clear blue eyes and my buddy standing beside my chair while I told them about Baby Jesus, I felt the true meaning of Christmas. I knew those babies loved and trusted me when they both went to sleep in my lap.

When they were put to bed my little buddy pointed to my lap and asked, "Can I sit up there while you talk about Jesus and Santa Claus coming in the front door with Rudolph and them deer's and smoke?"

I told him, "You better believe you can sit up here while I talk about them." It wasn't 5 minutes until he was gone, too. I turned to let his mother put him in bed and noticed she had tears in her eyes again. I told her she was going to get sick if she didn't stop that kind of stuff.

All she said was, "Deacon, you and Mrs. Balliew are something. I love you as much as my kids do, and

121

always will. What would I have done if I hadn't met you in the store? How in this world will I ever repay you two for this?"

The only reply I could muster was, "We love you, too. Let Inez put my pal to bed and you sit over here on the couch while we open our Christmas gifts. We want you to open yours first." I handed her an envelope, which she opened, and when she saw the $500.00 check she grabbed a towel to cry in. We didn't say anything to her for a few seconds—we knew it would not do any good.

When she did speak she said, "This is the most money I have ever had at one time in my life. Now I can find us a place to live by ourselves." I sat there wishing my good friends Clarence, Tommy and Wayne could be there to see the appreciation for their gift. I told the ladies I would go to my friend's house and get Santa Claus's gifts, and would meet them up stairs in a few minutes.

As I drove to my friend's house I thought about how those last few days were meant to happen and thanked the Lord for letting me see him do his work, especially on Christmas.

I am not kidding when I say this is and always

has been one of my favorite parts of the Christmas season: helping put the gifts under the tree. I guess it comes from my childhood anticipation, not feeling I could wait one more day. That feeling of not being able to go to sleep on Christmas Eve, tossing, tumbling and finally waking up and running to the Christmas tree to see what gifts were there.

We put many colorful toys and two baby dolls under our tree. The pretty pink dress, a red wagon, two tricycles, three sets of clothes and shoes each, a jacket each, toboggan caps, gloves, coloring books and crayons, small toys of many descriptions... the list went on. The children's mother said the kids had never gotten anything for Christmas before and would be spoiled by this one. That's when I started sniffling again.

On Christmas morning we got up, had breakfast and were sitting at the table, talking. Well, lets say the ladies were talking; I was sitting there getting edgier by the minute. I finally told the two of them I couldn't stand it any longer. "I'm going down stairs and wake our three up, get their attention and bring them upstairs."

All I had to do as open the squeaky bedroom

door and my little buddy's feet hit the floor. Questions poured out: "Did he, did Santa Claus come in the door last night?"

"We will have to wake up the girls, get them up and go upstairs and see if he did." My pal jumped on the bed and shook the older sister, shouting for her to "get up, he came in our door last night!"

She sat straight up in bed, wide-eyed; all the noise woke up the baby and had her crying, and down the stairs came Mrs. Balliew to pick up the baby.

"Did they wake you up? I'll give them a spanking if they scare you like that again," she told the little one. There was a mad scramble up the stairs; our young man Spunkie was already standing and rubbing his eyes, and saying something about Santa Claus. My new buddy just stood there looking like he was afraid to touch anything, not saying a word.

I was shocked when I saw that precious little girl pick up the pink dress first and hand it to her mother. After a little encouraging all three got busy playing with what Santa left for them and having a good time.

After the holidays all the people that made promises came through: the mother got an apartment and a job. Their apartment was furnished with help. My

124

little buddy got into kindergarten. Some of our neighbor friends along with Inez were faithful babysitters and the mother proved us right: with a little help she was a fantastic mother to those children.

Even after these many years when I think back, it stirs my emotions. When I think how much that mother loved those three kids, how trapped in that situation she was and how God in his wisdom sent a grouchy person with a headache, heartburn and sore finger at just the right time to meet her in the K-Mart.

We saw that little family almost every week for quite a while. All three of those children became like grandchildren to Inez and me. The mother later moved out of town because of getting married. Her new husband was a man who became a caring father to all three of her children, plus one of their own.

My little buddy is still my friend, but now he is married with one child and is a supervisor with a construction company. My little girl in the pink dress is married and lives in another town studying to be a nurse. She still has that pink dress and proved it a couple of Christmases ago when I visited her family.

The baby graduated from high school and is still at home, but is going to college to become a teacher.

125

Every time we see each other we always say "I love you." I am truly lucky and blessed to have been chosen to be loved by that family. The mother never fails to call me on birthdays, holidays and sometimes when she says, "I was thinking about you and wanted to let you know I love you."

Sometimes she will say, "I still have that hand towel I cried in, next to where I put my family Bible, and when things are not going well or just for the sake of it, I will get it out, sit and remember and things get a lot better. You might not believe it but I have never washed it. Deacon, you are something, you know that?"

"I sure am," I said. "I am the blessed man that got to know you and your crowd. Take care and don't forget I love you." We still see each other sometime during the Christmas holidays just to wish each other a Merry Christmas.

Each year since when I start feeling like Mr. Scrooge, and it never fails, I think of this family. It brings back the Christmas spirit—you better believe it.

Pictures I wanted to share...

Waiting for the bus

What snake? Snake! SNAKE!

Helping with the United Way campaign

First experience with the ocean and waves

Don't touch nothing on my desk!

Yearly visit to the County Fair

County Fair award winners

Some of our heroes

Santa comes by for a visit each year

Some of our community's Christmas gifts for forty young
people

131

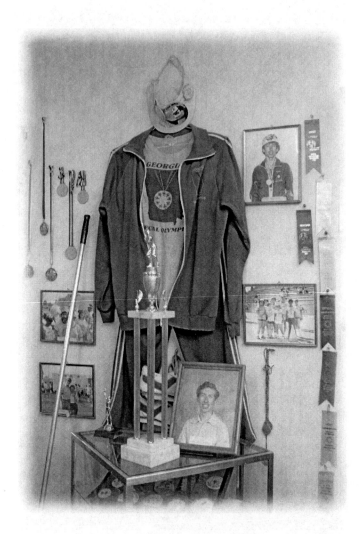

Curley's awards and memories

The Boy Who Chased the Wind

Mr. Webster, in his dictionary, describes a miracle as "a supernatural event" and in this case and in my mind he is absolutely right. I have since learned a lot more about this supernatural event, especially from the young man who could run.

I got to witness an instant in a young man's life, a few seconds that started one of my best friends on his journey to greater self-confidence, self-esteem, and being accepted. It started in a place called Brockport, N.Y., far from Calhoun, Georgia. I guess you can call this the rest of the story.

Jackie "Curley" Proctor, in the last several years, only sometimes has been willing to discuss with me the times in his life that were so troubling. When I say "several years" and "sometimes," that is exactly what I mean. Curley is a fellow that very seldom discusses negative subjects, especially about people or things that were part of his younger, troubled times.

I can understand now why my pal didn't like to have conversations with people. He told me, "I was afraid if I said anything, I would say the wrong thing, and they would laugh or make fun of me."

As a child, I also had to learn to tolerate some of the same feelings and emotions, and that helped me to understand our discussions and appreciate his frustrations. I asked him on several different occasions and got several answers as to why he thought those kids wouldn't let him run or play with them.

Once he recalled, "They sometimes called me 'retard' and ran me off; sometimes they said I smelled bad, and sometimes they hit me and run and chased me."

"When they said those things what did you do? Did you tell a teacher or your parents?" I asked.

"Sometimes at school when they hit me I cried, and at home when I felt bad I crawled under the bed and cried. I didn't tell nobody."

"Why?" I asked.

"Because I didn't think nobody would believe me. Sometimes they said if I told they would beat me up."

I said, "I guess you know now, you have shown a few things to all those boys and girls who make fun of, Curley."

"Yep, I sure did!"

I remember once when we were talking, I asked

134

Curley, "What do you think you showed those boys and girls, pal?"

"I showed them I was a champion runner and a good fellow," he said.

"Were any of them at the banquet that you, Ann and I went to with all the other runners? Do you ever see them any more?" I asked.

"Two of them was there and shook my hand and said I could run real fast. One of the girls hugged my neck, and sometimes when they see me now they shake my hand and say 'hello Curley'," he said, and smiled.

I knew I didn't need to question my pal any further. I knew I didn't want to know who those boys and girls were; besides, I believed Curley felt they knew they were wrong and in their way had apologized, which was just fine with him.

I'll bet, since the All Sports Banquet, that crowd has wished they hadn't treated Curley the way they had, and if it were possible would turn back the clock to those days and act differently.

In my almost 40 years of being friends of and loved by people who were supposed to be mentally retarded (the phrase "mentally challenged" was not coined at the time), I found so many people wanted to

135

feel pity for my friends.

In the beginning I admit I felt the same way, but I soon realized those individuals had talents and skills they didn't know how to exhibit. When given a chance, patience and love, their dreams and talents often became reality.

You probably will think I have gotten ahead of the real story when you read this. But I want readers to know it took years and many conversations to get those statements from Curley.

While I was sitting thinking about how to write the rest of this story, it was like reliving that time twenty-eight years ago; I can't think about those times without rekindling emotions that almost bring me to tears. It's been a long time since then and some of the details are sketchy but I remember vividly what I thought as I lay in bed at the end of that memorable day. "Lord, thank you; this is big time. You have allowed me to participate in and see one of your miracles."

I absolutely believe miracles happen. If someone suggests a miracle has happened and if you investigate, you will find love was involved and surrounding the event, and we all know love is a gift from God.

When I first met him, Jackie Proctor was a tall, skinny kid with a mop of hair that gave him the nickname "Curley" and a smile that would melt the hardest heart. I first met this smiling kid at the old Liberty School. At that that time it was being used as the first school for mentally challenged students in Gordon County.

The time Curley spent at Liberty School was tremendously important in his life. At that school were two young teachers: the first two teachers hired, just out of college, for the purpose of implementing a class for our community's mentally challenged students and others with special needs.

Calhoun City Schools hired Addie Perry and the Gordon County School system hired June Curtis. Time proved that these two teachers were excellent choices, young ladies who were both understanding and compassionate. They also had two assistants: a young, quiet, very capable and serious parent named Iris Parker and an old fellow named Deacon Balliew who had been asked by Calhoun City Schools Superintendent Mr. Vassa Cate to help get things off and running.

I had my doubts about how I could help, and I

told that to Mr. Cate.

"Deacon, the community knows you for what you have been doing with those mentally retarded fellows out at the Gordon County Training Center," he answered. "You'll be a big help to the school."

I wondered about that.

I'll not guess how many young lives these three ladies have touched; I know it would be in the thousands. All three are still very devoted educators who to this day help to brighten the lives and futures of hundreds of our community's special needs and troubled children.

I was very fortunate to be involved with them, and still consider them special friends. You can't be familiar with those three and not love them; I sure do.

I mention these three because of the years of caring and work that were instrumental in Curley's education, his learning social and living skills, that will benefit him for the rest of his life.

I gradually began to realize somehow a dream had grown in the cloudy world of that curly-headed 16-year-old boy's mind. I know it must have been God who brought the two of us together.

After getting to know Curley and gaining some

138

trust, I asked him one day if he ever thought of something he wanted very badly to do or dreamed about doing while he was going to school.

His answer was immediate, as if it had been memorized, rehearsed or had been on his mind for a long time: "I want to be a champion runner and run races. I can run real fast, too. And they wouldn't let me run with the rest of them boys."

"What boys?" I asked.

"Them boys at school and them kids at home."

With that statement alone, that he had a "dream." I knew it qualified him to become a friend of my wife Inez, myself and a group of mothers who had started a Boy Scout troop.

Our Scout troop was made up of young people who were being treated like life's misfits and rejects: the mentally handicapped, the physically handicapped and the abused and emotionally scarred, most with histories of social deprivation that horrify in the hearing.

Almost without exception, the largest segment of our group was made up of young people that traditional institutions were having trouble trying to help become successful. Some of them had been committed to institutions; institutions that were supposed to have the knowledge to help eliminate behaviors that society did not accept as normal.

I heard them tell stories that make me shudder even now, about how those professionals tried to help. Thank God we have come a long way (though we have a longer way to go) in realizing those young people have many skills that need to be found and nurtured.

I remember asking Curley at the time what those boys did that made him think they didn't want him to run with them. He didn't say anything, just lowered his head, smiled and looked away.

I didn't pursue the subject any further; I knew Curley well enough by then to know that further questions would be useless.

In 1976, when Jackie Proctor shared with me his secret dream, the first thing I decided to do, was go with him to the track for a workout with my son Glenn. Glenn was on the track team at Calhoun High School.

The two warmed up for a few minutes, stretching and jogging, and then it was time for the first run. I remember showing Curley how to line up and wait for me to give the signal to start.

I nearly fainted when that skinny kid broke from

the starting line. He could run like the wind! What I remember most about that day as I watched him as he ran, was that his head didn't move; all I saw moving was elbows and knees. His head stayed level the whole way.

I knew then I needed to help him find some way to run races like he had dreamed about. When I told him he was a good runner and asked him why he could run so fast, the answer was, "I like to run after the wind so I can feel it blowing in my face."

A few days later I went to see an old classmate and buddy of mine, Coach Lynn Walter, who at the time was the very successful track coach at Calhoun High School. I questioned him about Curley, and wondered aloud if he would qualify to compete for our high school.

After hearing Curley's story, Lynn said, "I'm sorry Deacon, but the boy doesn't meet the eligibility requirements."

He said he could give me some materials that explained a few basic stretching and training exercises and told me he would help any way he could, and especially with the next plan I discussed with him.

I have been involved with the Special Olympics

program since its beginning nationally, so with Curley in mind and with help I organized the Special Olympic Games in Gordon County. Jackie "Curley" Proctor, without his knowledge, was on his way to his dream.

I had shown Curley videos of Special Olympians involved in track and field events. Those videos had the young man excited and fired up; actually, fired up was an understatement. Suddenly Curley became very vocal, asking questions about what would happen if he won races.

The questions I will never forget were, "Will people make fun of me if I get beat running them races? If I don't win will they laugh at me? Do kids there get scared?"

"Mr. Curley Proctor, the answer to all your questions is absolutely not. Don't you know you are already a winner and don't have to be afraid of anyone making fun of you? When you decided to be a runner, you joined the Special Olympics. Do you remember standing out on that track while we were practicing the Special Olympians oath, making everybody a promise that you were going to do the best you could?

"Anyone who makes that kind of promise and keeps it is already a winner. If you race with some boys and they win, as long as you run as fast as you can, you may get beaten but won't lose. Then you can go practice to get better and try again. One day you will blow their doors off. I know you: you are never going to lose a race. You're only a loser if you don't do the best you can. You are going to make them beat you, because doing your best makes you a winner," I said.

I saw the smile that Curley was famous for, a smile that showed everyone he was comfortable with the situation at hand. Much later I learned that Curley used his smile as camouflage when he was afraid to show his true feelings. He told me years later, "I smile when I am happy, when I am sad, and when I don't know what to say."

So this is how it went for almost three years, two or three times a week. In the evenings after I got off from work, I would go by Curley's house and pick him up, and we would head downtown to the high school track to practice.

Curley could run the 200 meters in about 30 seconds when we first started. I thought about the advice Lynn had given me many times, and as I began to use those techniques, Curley's times gradually improved.

143

We didn't let Curley run as fast as he could very often. Lord, it's just like yesterday, as I sit here and think about this part of Curley's dream. One memory is very vivid: when the sun was shining, or it was bright outside I always squinted my one good eye. My other eye had been blinded by a long-ago accident and I would close it. That kept Curley puzzled at first, because he wondered if he had done something wrong.

I told him "When I look at you like that I've got the eagle eye on you, pal, especially when you slow down and start checking out the ladies."

I knew I had to be careful when explaining things to him; he had a constant fear of failure. He looked at me and grinned, and I knew then he was okay with that answer. I had discovered if he got scared or anxious about the least thing, his confidence level dropped and he would start worrying, sometimes wanting to stop for the day. But now a trust had developed and things were working well.

As the months flew by, a group of his friends would sometimes stop to watch him practice. It got so that almost everybody who came to the track to work out or walk knew Curley and what he was training to do. Sometimes it was hard to get him to practice, but

144

when the ladies jogged or walked past him on the track and said, 'Hey, Jackie! How's it going, handsome?" that usually would fire him right up and his motivation soared.

We participated in the Special Olympics program on a local and regional level the first year with Curley winning all his races. I had coached Curley to try to win every race he entered. The next year was another matter: Race as fast as you can. I began to see Curley run just fast enough to win. He had a wonderful disposition after winning a race, never boasting, just flashing that famous smile many times.

Two years passed, and Curley had competed in all local, regional and Georgia State Special Olympic competitions, winning in all of them. Then one day it came: an invitation to the International Special Olympic Games in Brockport, N.Y.

Our invitations stated that I was to be a coach for the state of Georgia and our Calhoun athlete Jackie Proctor was going to run in the 200-meter race for the United States of America.

I have to tell you, nerves, jitters and all kinds of other emotions were present before and after we boarded the plane for New York. Curley turned out to be mostly an "eyes closed, it is a long way down there, armrest gripper and for sure didn't like to sit by the window" airline passenger.

He wanted me to think he was asleep most of the time, but every time the plane hit a little turbulence the white-knuckled grip on the armrest gave me a different message.

When we arrived at Rutherford College in far-away New York, we found ourselves among the likes of Muhammad Ali, Eunice Shriver, and more celebrities than you could believe, along with hundreds of Special Olympians from around the world.

We were very busy that week with opening ceremonies practice at the stadium each day. We had very little time during the day to be together or to watch all the athletes practice. All we could do was discuss the day's events when we were in our dorm at night.

Curley's race was at two o'clock on Wednesday of that week. Waiting for his race was nerve-wracking for me, but he seemed to be having a ball, with not a sign of worry at all. It probably had something to do his being a hit with the young Irish ladies who, among others, shared our dorm building.

146

On the day of the race, a group of our Georgia athletes and coaches stood outside the chain-link fence in the last turn when the race started. It was the last race of the day. The pistol sounded and I saw the runners coming to the first turn. Curley was ahead of two or three at the start and had passed some others before the turn. In every race Curley had run he had always said to me, "I just run fast enough so I can beat them."

I had told Mr. "Just Fast Enough" Proctor the evening before his event, "Tomorrow is the time you don't run just fast enough, tomorrow is the day the judges will decide if you are a champion. You, my friend, have to beat everyone by a mile, then you just may be the champion. Do you understand, big boy? Tomorrow doors will be blown off, big time?"

"Yes sir, I'm gonna blow off them boys' doors tomorrow," he agreed, reaching out to shake my hand.

Having that statement in my mind didn't help me too much; I really didn't know if Curley understood. I was a nervous wreck. I found out later from the other coaches I sure showed it, with all the jumping, screaming and I don't know what else they witnessed from me.

At the midway point, he passed the runner for third place. We had always discussed in the last turn he should run flat out to the finish line, no matter how far ahead he was. I will never forget the sound those thousands of fans made; it was deafening, and all were on their feet, waving their arms and cheering.

There were two runners left a few feet in front of him. Curley pulled even with them. The crowd now was going even crazier. As Curley went by me I saw a smile that hadn't been there in any of his other races.

At that moment Curley Procter knew he was about to fulfill his dream of being a champion. He beat the last two runners by several yards.

I remember as Curley flew down the stretch, cold chills ran all over me. Lord, nothing had ever gotten to me like that. There was a miracle happening. A few seconds later, when I got close enough to see Curley, he was not talking to anyone. The crowd was still showing all its excitement, though.

Curley was simply shaking his head and showing that famous smile. I knew he had no idea he had won a world championship for Calhoun, Georgia. He knew he had won again in a different setting altogether; I believe the crowd noise was what really got to him.

148

When I got to the exit gate to meet Curley, he was shaking all over. One of the track officials with his arm around Curley looked at me and said, "Coach, look at this timer; this kid just ran that race in 22 seconds flat!"

I didn't know at the time how fast that was; all I knew was that the skinny kid from Georgia who could run like a deer had just won the race of his life. It was much later that I found out that his winning time had beaten our Calhoun High School track record.

I didn't know it when Curley crossed that finish line in Brockport, N.Y., but it would be his last race. That night he came to me before the Recognition Banquet for the Athletes. He was looking at his gold medal, and he asked "Mr. Balliew, am I gonna have to run any more?"

I answered him in a way I thought he would understand. "Curley, you know our dream of you being a champion runner we talked about so many times? Well, that dream came true out there on that track today. There are no more races you need to run. You have beaten all the fastest runners up here.

"You are the best in the world; all those screaming people in the stands that saw you race know they were watching the best. There's no one today faster or better than you."

"I'm the best. I'm the champion. When do we go home?" he asked.

That night at the reception, Jackie "Curley" Proctor dressed in his gold medal and his Georgia state uniform met many celebrities. My back was turned when "Superman" Christopher Reeves walked up, looked at the gold medal, and told him he did a great job that day. That really got his attention.

Curley grabbed my arm with a nervous jerk. I saw him blush for the first time as he looked at me and said, "That was him. That was the real Superman, the one I saw in the movies!"

We didn't know what was happening at home. We only made three phone calls home about the successful trip, one each to Curley's family, my family, and WJTH Radio. I guess three was the magic number, because it seemed everybody in Calhoun knew our track star when we got home on that Saturday. The radio interviews put the icing on the trip.

What really got my attention was when Curley and I were alone, and he said, "I'm afraid. Will you tell me what to say to them people? I might say the wrong

150

thing."

That statement brought back a memory of a comment he had made to me a couple of years before. I had asked him why he wouldn't talk to people—how he feared saying the wrong thing.

I told Curley that a champion couldn't say anything wrong, because people wanted to hear every word he had to say and whatever he said would be right. He did great with only a few words: "I run real fast up there in New York."

I guess one of the most unforgettable moments in my life, and I've had many, was explaining to Curley that he was invited to the All Sports Banquet at Calhoun High School. It was the first time I had heard of any Special Olympian being invited. Coach D.A. Richardson, one of the most innovative coaches I have ever had the opportunity to know, knew Curley and the long road he had to travel to become a true champion. He invited Curley (and his date) to be recognized along with our community's other winning athletes, and honored as one of Calhoun and Gordon County's finest athletes.

After I had the opportunity to introduce Curley and his date Ann Edwards to all the other award recipients and guests, to tell them the story of Curley's long journey to that day on that Brockport track, he got a standing ovation from all present. When the banquet was over, everyone there came by, shook his hand and congratulated him.

A while back I was talking to a friend of mine, Jeff McBee, about Curley's story and what he had accomplished. In the 1980s Jeff attended Calhoun High School and was a three-time state champion in the 400-meter run, which earned him an athletic scholarship to the University of Georgia in track and field.

While at the university he accomplished his dream of becoming a NCAA All-American in track and field. In our discussions Jeff said, "I understand exactly how Curley felt in that last race, and why he was smiling. It's hard to put in words but I think he knew that all the hard work was suddenly going to be behind him, and he was about to accomplish the thing he had worked all that time for, to be a champion.

"He will always know those feelings; he might not know how to explain them. When looking back at the times spent on all those tracks that he had to keep his dream in focus not only with his eyes, but his mind and heart also, to have accomplished what he did. It

152

was his time to give it all he had.

"It got lonesome sometime on those tracks even with all the crowds around. I know the feeling. And I bet most people don't know that the time Curley ran back then would still win most of high school races today."

Jeff also said any coach who knows sprinting will tell you that the description of Curley's form was that of a natural sprinter. I know there are lots of runners with good form but to know what to do with it is a whole different story. Curley's ability to use his form to harness speed was a God-given talent.

When we were almost home from the sports banquet that night, I asked Curley how he felt. His answer? "I'm done running now, and I feel real good, too."

I wondered if one or more of the young people he had mentioned as hassling him were at the banquet that night, and how they felt to shake the hand of a person they knew was now a true champion, the skinny kid they made fun of, before.

I knew at that moment what he had meant on our plane ride home from Brockport. After we were in the air for a few minutes, clutching his gold medal,

Curley said, "I wish them boys could have been up there at that race track, and heard all them people hollering and clapping their hands."

I don't think he realized he was talking; when I asked him about what he said, he just smiled. There were very few words from Curley on the way home; our champion was sure afraid of flying.

I did lots of thinking on the flight though, about how the Lord has blessed me with this opportunity, how I got to watch a young man in his own way repay every one of us for our help and encouragement. And maybe even those "boys" will get the message, too. I knew that Curley didn't have a vindictive bone in his body.

I believe in the depths of his mind and in his heart, that he knew in his own way he had gotten a profound point across. I also thanked the Lord for allowing me to see one of His miracles performed.

When God allowed this to happen to me it made me an even more devoted believer in people with challenges and how they can become winners at something if given a chance.

Those 28 years have passed like a flash. I've been asked by people in the community and around the state what has happened since his gold-medal-winning race: "Where is Curley? What is he doing today?"

After he completed all the requirements at Gordon Central High School for a special education diploma, he went to work with his father in Calhoun, Georgia at Proctor's Garage. He was still a very shy young man, and it was hard for him to adjust and learn how to relate to strangers.

I can remember the times his Dad placed him in situations where he had to respond to people's questions. He learned fast how to use his infectious smile to give him time to muster a response.

He has become a vital part of the Proctor Garage operation. He is a jack-of-all-trades, but answering the phone is where Curley Proctor excels, smiling and telling about things going on around the shop.

I was told Curley knows very well how to help keep the peace among his "garage family." He keeps the shop floors immaculately clean and will only complain when the guys toss something on "his floor," with the look in his eyes letting the mechanics know they are causing him unnecessary work.

He will make sure the mechanics are looking, gaze at his problem and then stare at the garbage can for a second before he continues his work. Curley knows with that kind of wisdom, a fellow doesn't have to embarrass his pals with advice.

At knowing where the required used parts have been stored, Curley Proctor is a genius. According to the mechanics, that knowledge is a gift that saved customers hundreds of dollars.

Curley has been accepted as the beacon to look for when visiting Proctor's Garage. If you see my pal's smile you will understand why.

When I told Curley I planned to rewrite this story and asked if there was anything he wanted me to tell anyone, he shook his head "no" very slowly.

"Why?" I asked.

"I don't know nothing to say to them."

As I thought about his answer, he was 100 percent right. He didn't have to say anything; he said all he needed to say on that distant track in New York 28 years ago.

I also asked Curley again why he never ran on the track anymore; his answer was clear and sudden: "I didn't want to."

I believe he really meant by that statement that he had nothing else to prove by running. I can assure you he really meant it too; he has not set a foot on a track to race since then, except to light the Olympic flame at a few of our local Special Olympics games.

I mentioned earlier about the friendship that developed between the two of us. I can truthfully say that Jackie "Curley" Proctor is one of my best friends, and it is a friendship that has continued to grow and will last our lifetimes.

Everyone who comes in contact with Curley Proctor likes him instantly. He is just Curley, a "take him as he is" kind of fellow and that's all that matters to him. He is still shy in his own special way, but that smile of his will remove any barriers that could cause a person not to like him.

I have seen many dreams come true because my family firmly believes that if you can dream a realistic dream and are willing to pay the price no matter what it takes, it can happen.

Thank you Lord, for the kid who chased the wind and for helping me to understand that dreams can really come true.

Cotton's Bag of Marbles

It's now been many years since I first saw Cotton riding an old bicycle with a wobbling front wheel, a bike that had seen its better days years before, pedaling through the Red Bud community.

For several months I watched this skinny, pathetic-looking kid: unkempt and under-nourished, lonesome, seldom ever smiling. He had the sad eyes of a kid looking for something to do, or something to care about, and who couldn't find it. When I talked with him I could feel and see the loneliness by the look on his face.

In the beginning I never saw evidence that he had any young friends in the community. Cotton went about his business alone, seldom talking to anyone.

Once while visiting his school I had the opportunity to talk to one of his teachers who said, "He attempts to be friendly with the other children but most of them shy away from him, or they say something to make fun of him that hurts his feelings and many times an argument or fight develops.

"He looks unkempt much of the time, and his

personal hygiene is pretty bad. The kids made fun of him calling him 'stinky' and 'beggar'. He really is a sad child. I have referred him to special education."

Most of the times when I saw Cotton, I made an effort to talk with him. We got to know each other fairly well, usually while we were around Mr. French's store.

He was an expert at something that was a marvel to me. I never saw him when he didn't always have a few cents in his pocket he made by collecting discarded Coke bottles, which were redeemable at Mr. French's store for two cents each.

For a 10-year-old kid in those days, that was pretty good money. Five empty bottles equaled a candy bar; several more meant the big time: a Coke and a candy bar, with a little extra change to be saved for those bad days when he couldn't find any throwaways or get people to let him have the Coke bottles they had at home.

Cotton could be seen walking and pushing his bike along most of the Red Bud community's roads and streets, with his eagle eyes looking for discarded soft drink bottles.

Cotton was also one of the best I had ever seen

at using his skill of what I called mooching, "Do you have any old Coke bottles I can have or can I borrow a dime to buy me something to eat? I'll pay you back, I promise." Looking at that sad face, I fell for his mooching several times.

I had just started working with the Gordon County Juvenile Court. While on a visit into the Red Bud community to see some kids I had on probation, I saw Cotton rounding the corner of a house at a dead run, being chased by a man with a leaf rake in his hands. The man wore loose, dirty jeans tucked into a pair of rubber boots, with an undersized oil-stained sweater over an equally dirty T-shirt, neither of which quite covered his fat stomach.

When I stopped in the road next to his house he lowered his rake and looked at me suspiciously. A red face and matted dark brown hair made him look like a crazy man, but his eyes, glaring, sunken and dark, showed his anger.

I loudly said "Hello!" and waited for a response. The man narrowed angry eyes and strode towards me.

"Are you the law?" he yelled, flailing his arms. "If you are, get this little thief out of here before I knock his brains out!"

At that time a neighbor lady joined in. "Why can't you leave that boy alone?" she cried from the window. "What's the mater with you, Newt? What has got into you? All Cotton was trying to do was help you rake the yard."

I asked Cotton why he was running and why the man was threatening him with the rake.

Cotton said, "I don't know what he meant. He was hollering at me and calling me a stealer and I was scared, and I didn't do nothing neither so I took off running. I guess it's cause he don't like me."

I could tell by Cotton's gaze he was puzzled and not the kind of a kid who would try to make someone that angry. He wasn't eager to continue helping old Newt, either.

I was entirely confused about what I had seen and asked Newt what seemed to be the problem. It had been a long time since I had seen a grown man act in such a way.

Newt asked me who I was and after I told him, he gave me the story. It was obvious he still was not very happy with Cotton.

"That stinking kid has stole from me for the last time. Every time he comes to our house he steals something; last time he stole three ham and biscuits I was going to take to work for supper."

The man's wife, now standing on the porch, said, "Now Newt, I told you that boy must have been hungry or he wouldn't have took your biscuits, and anyway the dog could have got them."

"Are you crazy, woman? How in the heck could that mutt get in the kitchen anyhow?" Newt yelled, then said to me, "Mr. Government Man, look in that darn kid's back pocket and you will see my plug of Red Man chewing tobacco he took. It's still sticking out."

I looked, and as sure as the devil, Cotton had Newt's plug sticking out of his pocket. Before I could speak, Cotton said, "I was just holding it for him."

Mrs. Newt looked at Cotton and said, "In your back pocket... young man, that is not a likely story and I'm disappointed in you."

I told Cotton to get his bike so we could put it in my car trunk, then to get in my car and I would take him home. I told him that he was not in any trouble and to give Newt back his tobacco, which he did. It was obvious that Newt was still aggravated. He snatched the tobacco out of Cotton's hand and told him, "You little thief, get yourself out of here and don't ever come back. Stay away from here, do you hear?"

Cotton looked at me and said, "I don't like chewing tobacco. I tried to chew it once and got bad sick in my stomach and threw up a bunch."

As I started to leave Mrs. Newt told me she would like to talk to me. After Cotton was in the car she told me she was really worried about him. She said Cotton's family was mean to him, that his Daddy was a drunk and often beat on him and his mother, and would run them out of the house late at night.

She had seen belt marks and welts from whippings on his arms and legs several times, that I needed to check it out, and for sure not to tell the family she said anything. After assuring her that I would not say anything about her, I got into my car and we started to Cotton's house.

On our way Cotton told me, "That old Newt, he hates kids. My mama says to stay away from him."

"What's the matter with him?" I asked.

"I think he's crazy or something. Ain't none of the kids who likes him; sometimes he asks me to help him do something and when I try to help him he fusses, tells me lies and don't pay me for helping him and just laughs when I ask him to pay me."

164

"Why do you help him then?"

"Sometimes he will pay me a dollar but other times he just fusses and says he will pay me the next time I help him," the boy said.

Cotton told me where he lived and gave me directions to his house As we pulled into his driveway I saw what appeared to be a fight in his yard. A large man with a beard and long hair had someone on the ground with his fist drawn back to strike them.

To my amazement, his target was a small lady lying on the ground with her arms covering her face. As I was getting out of the car, Cotton jumped out and ran toward them, screaming, "Get off of her, and leave her alone; she didn't do nothing to you!"

I grabbed Cotton by the shirt as the man got off the woman. He yelled, "Who called the law?" and he broke and ran for the woods beside the trailer.

After looking at the woman and seeing how small she was I thought, "The woods are just where that guy needs to be."

In a way I was proud of Cotton. I had never expected to see that kind of heroic behavior out of him, and felt sorry for him when I saw the tears in his eyes.

165

Cotton looked at me and said, "He is always doing that to my mama. My mama never does nothing to him."

As he was helping his mother brush the dirt and leaves off her clothes, Cotton made a statement that I knew he meant: "I'll kill him, I mean it. I will kill him for doing that to you, mama. I can't stand to see him do that to you no more. I hate him!"

Cotton's mother told him he shouldn't talk that way around strangers, that his daddy was just a little mad.

"He ain't no stranger; he's Deacon Balliew. I see him at school all the time. He is the one who helps kids that is in trouble, just like that policeman in Cherokee helped me," Cotton said.

I heard a motor starting in the woods and looked at the mother when she said, "That's his daddy, leaving like he always does after we have trouble."

I asked her if he was drinking, hoping he was so I could radio the Sheriff's Department and get him in jail.

"He's not drinking this time," she said.

"He's probably smoking that old pot; he gets mad every time he drinks or smokes that stuff," Cotton said.

166

"What in the world made him act like he did when we drove up and why was he fighting with you?" I asked.

"He don't need no reason to do bad stuff, he's crazy," Cotton said. "I hope he will be gone a long time like he was the other day."

I saw that he was hurting and thought I would try to help him. I asked the mother if Cotton was right, and she agreed.

"Anything I can do to help you guys?" I asked as I noticed her left eye starting to swell and darken. "Lady, you need to swear out a warrant for your husband for doing this stuff to you," I said.

"It will be alright. My friend lives down the road. We can stay with them if anything else happens; we will be ok," she tried to reassure me.

I looked at Cotton who was nodding his head and agreeing, which made me feel a little easier. I told him to behave, that I would see him later and told his mother I would be back to see her soon and left.

As I drove away, I realized that I hadn't told Cotton's mother why I was at their house in the first place. I didn't think it was the time to tell her about her son and the problems with Mr. Newt.

My mind was on a kid and his mother and the threats he made about hurting the father. From my experience with kids, I knew that he meant those threats when he made them, and one day if things didn't change he would probably try carrying them out.

I decided to start seeing him at school as soon as school started. School had been out for the summer break and would be starting back in a few days; I went by to see the principal.

I knew the principal would be in his office. I had talked to him early that morning about two other children that I would be working during with the coming year.

When I spoke with the principal, I found that Cotton had an explosive temper and was in fights quite often. They usually started when someone said something that hurt his feelings. He seemed to carry a chip on his shoulder all the time, had poor self esteem and kids picked on him regularly because of his appearance and the way he acted.

The principal told me, "Every time I've had Cotton in my office, he gets emotional and cries, and I feel the boy is genuinely sorry for his behavior. I'll be watching him very close this year because I'm worried
168

about his mental health."

I asked the principal if he had had any dealings with the boy's family and was told, "That boy's father is a tyrant. He rants and raves every time he's been in my office. I quit calling them when the boy gets in trouble. The mother was quiet as a church mouse when they were in here; I knew by the way she acted she was terribly afraid of him. I suspected the father was abusing the boy and probably the mother too. I hope you get involved with Cotton's family; they remind me of one you have worked with before."

I knew exactly the family he was referring to and thought, "Man, do I dread getting involved with another crazy mixed up family like them again." But I was getting to really like Cotton, and for his sake I would get involved.

Driving back to my office, I kept hearing the principal's words over and over again: every time Cotton was in his office he cried, that he thought the boy was genuinely sorry for this behavior and the kids make fun of him a lot.

I knew I was going to be seeing him. I thought he seemed like a pretty nice kid and I hoped we could keep our relationship on track. I would find out next week when school started.

It was just before lunch on Monday when I got the phone call. The police officer said, "Deacon, do you remember that kid I told you about last week, the one that was shoplifting at the drug store?"

"I sure do… why?"

"Well we got him again at the same drug store, and as last time they don't want to charge him with shoplifting. I need some help."

"How old is he?" I asked.

"He's 10 years old and said he knew you, that you were nice. Can you believe that? Are you losing your touch?"

"I'll be there in a few minutes," I told him, and left the office. When I got to the drug store, I saw a little fellow sitting in the police car. When I neared the car I was surprised: there sat Cotton looking very shy and with tears in his eyes.

He had been rubbing his eyes and the dust that had accumulated on his face had gotten wet and smeared across his face. He was a sight to see. I looked in the back seat of the police car and said, "Cotton, what in the world? And how did you get to town?"

"I rode my bike here."

"All the way from Red Bud?" I asked. It was a good 10-mile ride

I looked around and to my surprise, there next to the shrubbery sat his dilapidated bike that a few days before I had seen in Red Bud.

I talked with the drug store proprietor and was informed that they would not charge him this time because of his age but would the next time it happened.

"All that kid takes is food, crackers and the like, not candy like most kids take," he said, adding that he was banned from the store from now on.

I told the policeman I would take Cotton with me and asked if he would help me put his bike in my trunk.

The officer handed me the items he had removed from Cotton's pockets: a pocketknife with only one blade (broken), a key and a small tobacco sack full of marbles.

"This is the same bag of marbles he had in his pocket the last time I saw him. He must like marbles," the officer said, handing all except the knife back to Cotton.

As we left the store, Cotton asked where we were going and I told him I didn't know. I told him I could

171

take him to the Youth Detention Center, a place that was almost like a jail, where we had to put kids who were a threat to the community.

He asked me what a threat was. I told him, "A threat is someone who stole once, and made a policeman a promise that he wouldn't steal again… but got caught doing it a second time. Then when a Juvenile Court Officer thinks he probably will steal again, the Juvenile Court Officer decides to put him in the Youth Detention Center to protect people's stuff.

"I guess I will have to take you to the YDC or I can take you home after you make me a promise that you will not steal again. But you and your mother will have to come to my office one day this week and then we will decide what we will have to do about your stealing."

In an instant he told me he wanted to be put in the YDC. I know he couldn't have thought about it very much before he made that decision.

When I asked why he said, "My daddy will get real mad and whup me bad."

I had seen kids in the past that had rather be locked up than face a parent, knowing they were going to get severe consequences. And almost every time a

172

kid made the decision to get locked up, things were very bad for him at home.

After what I had seen out of his parents I decided to go back to the police department to talk to Cotton and the police officer again. I needed to find out what the officer knew about Cotton's parents.

While waiting for the police officer to return to the station we had time to talk. I asked him why he didn't want to go home.

He said, "I told you before … I'm afraid my daddy will whup me."

"That's usually what happens to some kids when their parents find out their kid gets caught stealing. You know that, don't you? I asked him.

"Yeah I know that, but my daddy whups you a bunch of times; some times he won't hardly stop either, and will whup you bunches of times for one thing you done."

Trying to understand I asked, "What do you mean a bunch of times?"

"He will whup you and make you go to bed and will get up in the morning and whup you again."

He had tears in his eyes; my experience told me I needed to look out for this little fellow. Those tears I saw weren't simply playing for pity as I had seen many times in the past.

When the police officer arrived at the station, I asked what happened the last time he saw Cotton and how he acted. The officer told that he had released him to his mother who walked up while he was talking to him.

He did remember the mother telling him that he was in trouble and she hoped his daddy didn't find out about him stealing because he would be real mad and he knew what would happen then. She then told the boy to get in the car.

The officer also told me that the mother turned pale, seemed very nervous and scared and seemed like she was about to cry. He didn't like what he saw then; that's the reason he had called me about what happened this time.

I thanked him and told him he was right to do that and that I was going to check things out. I went back to where Cotton was and told him to come with me, that I was taking him home.

While in the car I told him that I was not going to tell his daddy at this time but couldn't say what I would do later. On the way home I told Cotton I was

174

going to let him out close to his home, but not right in front of it. I asked why everybody was so afraid of his daddy.

"Cause he gets real mad all the time and hollers real loud at everybody."

I asked him if his mother was as afraid of his daddy as he was. "Yep, she is, and I hate him for that. If he don't stop I'm going to kill him."

I knew I needed to hurry with my visit with the mother. As we drove by the area where we could see the trailer and where Cotton's daddy parked the truck. We saw that the truck was parked in the woods.

I told Cotton that his mama needed to call me as soon as possible, and not to tell anybody except his mama that he was in a little bit of trouble. He agreed. I let him out of the car a little ways from his drive and watched him start pedaling that old bicycle towards home.

I thought, "I'm going to see that Santa brings that fellow a new bike for Christmas."

I began to sympathize with Cotton. His life must be miserable living with a man like his dad seemed to be. It went through my mind that Cotton's daddy was beginning to force me to make decisions I don't like to make. Having to let a little fellow like Cotton out of the car, away from home so he wouldn't be seen getting out of my car, did not give me a good feeling.

I decided I would go back out there the next day, and if the dad was gone, I was going to stop and see Cotton and his mother.

The next day was Tuesday and school started on Friday. It would give me a chance to tell the mother that I was going to see Cotton at school and not at home. I also needed to discuss Cotton's trip to town with her, and his shoplifting at the drug store again.

As usual, I thought a prayer for the Lord to give me wisdom and knowledge to make the right decisions and say the right things. I was worried about Cotton and his mama.

Luck was with me the next day. I noticed the dad's truck headed towards town as I drove through Red Bud. This would give me a few minutes with the family. I pulled into the driveway and a pack of dogs met me, showing their teeth and snarling... not a good sign for a stranger who's visiting.

I noticed the mother walking out of the trailer calling the dogs and they suddenly disappeared under the trailer. I asked the mother if it was okay for me to

176

get out of the car; I couldn't see the dogs but I had no doubt they were under that trailer.

She nodded, but she asked, "Is everything all right? Is there any trouble?"

I told her that everything was okay. I had come to talk to her and Cotton for a few minutes while the father was not at home. She told me that Cotton was down at the neighbor's house and I was welcome to go by and talk to him if I needed to.

I told her, "Lady, that fight you and your husband had the other day was not a pretty sight to see. What caused it? Does he argue that way with you a lot?"

She nodded and said, "I just wish Cotton didn't see so much of him being mad."

I told her that I was worried about Cotton hurting his dad. She said she was worried about that, too.

"Do you have any kind of guns or anything around the house that Cotton could use to hurt your husband?" I asked.

The mother said, "There used to be a shotgun but it went missing a long time ago. I think someone stole it or my husband sold it. It was my daddy's old shotgun and I hated losing it."

I told her about Cotton riding his bike to town, shoplifting at the same drug store, what the police officer said to me, and finally about bringing him home and letting him out so no one would see us.

She told me that Cotton told her about it. They were going to have to come to town to the courthouse and talk to me about it. Cotton had been upset—he didn't want to get locked up in ·the YDC, but he wanted to know what that place was like.

I asked her, "Can you get to town without Cotton's father knowing about it? I don't want him to know about it right now."

She said, "Thank you, Deacon Balliew; it would be bad for Cotton if his daddy found out. He would probably get another hard whipping. His daddy don't believe in talking. He says talking don't do no good, only a whipping will teach a kid a lesson, but he don't know when to stop and will whip him too hard. I can get my neighbor to bring me tomorrow. Cotton's daddy will be going to Ellijay and will be gone all day. It will be good for Cotton to know what happens to a kid when he leaves home without permission and steals. He is getting too big for this britches."

178

I told her to be in my office in the courthouse at 10 a.m. and if she couldn't make it to call me.

I got to the office at 8:30 the next morning and saw both of them sitting in the hallway. I asked them why they were in the courthouse so early and the mother told me that the neighbor had to go to work at 8 a.m. and they had to ride with him. "Where is his father?" I asked.

"He went to Ellijay last night and won't be back until late this evening," the mother replied.

I had two big reasons to have them come by my office. I wanted both to know what Cotton had done could get him time in Juvenile Court, and if he shoplifted another time he would have to face the judge.

When I told Cotton that the judge could take him away from his family, "What does that mean?" asked Cotton.

"It means that the judge could send you off," I told him.

Cotton began to cry. I told him that he was not going to court this time, but next time if he kept getting in trouble. He continued crying and his mother asked him why he was crying.

Cotton said, "If I have to be sent off to that place I can't help you no more. I told him I wanted to be sent off, because I don't want to live at home no more."

"Is that why you are crying, because you don't want to live at home any more? You want to be sent some place?" his mother asked.

Cotton stopped crying, looked down at the floor, got quiet, and wouldn't respond to our questions. I asked him to go out and sit in the hall while I talked to his mother.

I asked, "Lady, you do realize you have a situation at home that causes Cotton to get very angry. I can tell you, that boy will someday try to hurt your husband if he keeps on fighting and hurting you. Can't you stop those fights?"

"He ain't my husband; we just live together. We have lived together a little while."

"You mean he is not Cotton's father? Cotton told me that he was his daddy. And if he is not your husband, why in the world do you live with him and take what I saw out at your house the other day?"

I also asked the mother if she would mind going to sit in the hall and send Cotton back in so he and I could talk.

I knew that this was as the principal had said—a very troubled family. From the way Cotton acted I could tell he had no one to understand and listen to his concerns. I sure hoped he would talk and listen to me.

"Cotton, do you really understand what we talked about when your mother was in here with you? Do you understand that your attitude will play a big part in the decision I have to make? And do you know you can worsen your problems that you have created for yourself with the decisions you made? You have created a situation that is serious with what you did: shoplifting, leaving home without permission, and especially your threats to do harm to your dad."

"I heard mama tell you he ain't my daddy and I hate him and wish I didn't have to live there no more," Cotton said.

We had a long discussion about the man that lived in the trailer with him and his mother. It was very obvious that I was going to have to talk with the man and see if I could help Cotton work out his frustrations.

I changed the subject and began discussing his school and the problems he was having there last year. When I asked him how he liked going to school he

181

said, "I like school pretty good, but I don't like to go because some of the kids are mean to me."

"How are they mean to you?"

"They make fun of me and sometimes won't let me go to the bathroom; one of them sometimes tells me they are going to put my head in the commode so they can wash the lice out of my hair. They tried one time and I ran away from them," Cotton said, getting teary eyed.

I asked him if he had any friends at school and was told he had just one best friend and what his name was. His friend would make the boys leave him alone sometimes.

I asked him if he told the principal about the boys that were causing him trouble. He said, "I told him once, but they told me if I told again they would beat me up and all of them shoved me around and made me fall in the hall and bump my head on the wall and made a big knot on it. I wish I could change schools. My mama said she might take me out of that school and put me in another."

I asked him if he wanted me to talk to the boys and maybe their parents, but he said that he wanted to try to get them to stop, himself. "What about your dad, did he try to help?" I asked.

"All he would say was to beat them up or get something to get them with. I can't beat up all them boys," he said.

I could see in his eyes that he was a troubled kid. Some way or another I had developed a way of looking in a kid's eyes to see what was going on, and I was seldom wrong. I could see sadness, loneliness, depression, fear and a lot of anger. Cotton was a very sad 10-year-old little boy.

As Cotton moved around I heard what I thought was marbles clinking together in his pocket. When I asked about them, Cotton informed me that he liked to shoot marbles, and could shoot them pretty good, too.

"Let me see your marbles," I said.

With a smile, he took out his bag of marbles and

started placing them on my desk one at a time; his stories about some of them were fantastic. He was extremely proud of what he called his lucky lagging taw and that he never used it to shoot.

After several enjoyable minutes discussing terms like cat eyes, agates, dubs, taw line, knuckling down and playing for keeps, I asked, "How and where did you learn about marbles and learn to shoot them?"

"My grandpa showed me how when I was a little boy and I'm pretty good at shooting them, too."

"Cotton, when I was a kid I was a marble shooter and was a pretty good one too, and when we get a chance we will have to shoot some," I told him.

I saw a smile on his face like I hadn't seen before.

"Do you shoot with knuckles on or off the ground? How big of a ring did you like to shoot in?" he asked. I was surprised at his knowledge of a game I hadn't played in many years, much less heard about lately.

"We will see when we start shooting. I'm not going to let a little kid marble-shooter blow my doors off; I am going to practice some," I said.

"You can't use a log roller *(an oversized marble)*.

You will have to use a regular taw," he said, leaving me the impression he had a knowledgeable teacher.

Marbles, I thought. Who would have believed that could be the thing that had broken the ice between the two of us? We exchanged smiles and agreed we were going to shoot marbles soon.

I was beginning to feel some relief as we talked, and the smile I saw was wonderful. I felt Cotton was developing some trust in me.

As he put his marbles back in the Dukes tobacco bag, I told him I was going to wait on making a decision about court and seeing the judge. I was going to give him a chance to prove to me and everybody else what kind of fellow he was. "Now go out into the hall and tell your mother to come back into my office."

When Cotton got up to go to the hall he reached and shook my hand; that was a shock to me. I told him that when two fellows shook hands they were buddies.

That's when he looked at me with tears in his eyes and said, "Mr. Balliew, you sure are one of my buddies and I'm gonna keep my promise to you."

I said, "Brother Cotton, you are my buddy too. We'll have to talk about shooting marbles again pretty soon."

"Yep!" he said, smiling, and like a flash he was gone. Before his mother came in I thought, "That kid must not have anybody to make him know he really is a special kid."

His mother stepped into the office and asked, "What happened? He came out there and said he liked you, that you are a good man and that you was his friend."

I told his mother, "I don't know, lady; I think it had something to do with his bag of marbles."

I remember thinking that I had accomplished what I wanted, and that was to develop a beginning friendship or at least some trust. I did what I do most times when things are and are not going my way—I thought a quiet prayer. "Thanks for the help, Lord; you know what it will take to help this little guy. I sure do like that little fellow. Help me Lord with this situation I have gotten myself into. Amen."

After lunch I went back to see the principal of Cotton's school. I wanted to see what all his teachers had to say about him. The principal got Cotton's permanent records and began to read and what we saw was a complete surprise.

In a Cherokee, N.C. school his first grade teacher

wrote, "Cotton is a bright, inquisitive child with a ready laugh. He does his work neatly and has good manners... he is a joy to be around." His second grade teacher wrote, "Cotton is an excellent student, well liked by his classmates, but is troubled because his father has a terminal illness and life at home must be a struggle."

His third grade teacher wrote, "Cotton continues to work hard but his father's death has been hard on him. He tries to do his best but his mother doesn't show much interest lately and his home life will soon affect him if some steps aren't taken."

The next entry was recorded by our school system's fourth grade teacher who wrote, "Cotton is withdrawn and doesn't show much interest in school. He sleeps in class and doesn't have many friends. He is often tardy and could become a problem."

The principal and I sat in silence for a few seconds. Finally he said, "Deacon, I had no idea. We have lots of work to do."

"Yes, we do, and I will help this family," I replied.

While we had the file I got Cotton's history, which I knew had all his family members' names and also his stepfather's name—who I knew was not really

187

his stepfather. There was another surprise: his grandfather had passed away in the past year.

No wonder that little guy was so depressed. Who in his life cared about him? His father gone, his grandfather gone, he lived with a raving tyrant and his mother didn't have the capability of helping the situation very much. No wonder he rode those Red Bud roads on that old bike, looking so sad.

As I sit here and write this I can feel the emotions I felt that day long ago. That little fellow with that bag of marbles was carrying a heavy load, but with the Lord's help, we helped lighten it.

As I drove back to the office I started thinking about the man who lived with Cotton and his mother. His last name I knew very well; I had been involved with several juveniles with the same last name.

I decided to do a criminal background check on that name. I was standing next to the Sheriff's dispatcher who was doing the background check when she said, "Bingo! Man, look here, Deacon!"

I looked at the printout and saw that the man who was living with Cotton and his mother was a prison escapee from North Carolina who had several more charges pending and was considered dangerous.

188

Later that day I watched as our Sheriff's deputies left to arrest him.

When they arrived back at jail with him in shackles, we looked at each other and he said, "Balliew, take care of that Cotton boy who lives with me; he is a pretty good kid," and asked the arresting officer to let him talk to me for a second.

When we were alone he told me, "I couldn't find it but I think Cotton has his grandpa's shotgun hid in the woods and I'm afraid he would hurt himself or someone else with it. Maybe he will tell you; I think he likes you."

"How do you know me?" I asked.

"Everybody knows you," he said and smiled. "Cotton's mother told me about you. I'll see you in about 20 years if I'm lucky—them other charges might get me more time."

I thought, "I sure hope so." Anybody with that kind of temper didn't need to be in society. He was in prison for attempting to kill someone and had the same kind of charges pending. No wonder Cotton's mother was so afraid of him and took those beatings.

I knew I needed to go out to Red Bud and see Cotton and his mother to assure them that we would help them if they needed us.

On my way out there, half way between Red Bud and Calhoun I spotted our boy Cotton on his way to Calhoun again, pedaling that old bike. I stopped and put that bike in my trunk again; it went in pretty easy. It should have; I'd had enough practice doing it.

In the car I asked Cotton where he was headed and in a few words knew I had his trust. Smiling from ear to ear, he said, "I was coming to see you, Mr. Balliew, and tell you the police got him and took him to jail and told my mama that he would not be back for bunches of years."

"Does your mother know where you are?"

"Nope, I couldn't wait; them police told us you was the one who had found out about him and the reason he was going back to jail. Mama was trying to get our truck cranked and told me to stay down at our neighbors, but I couldn't wait! Mr. Balliew, I'm happy he is gone and I had to come tell you."

I can remember this like it happened yesterday. We sat silent for a minute on the way to his house, and I again thought a prayer of thanks for all the help God had given me in this case.

All this happened in about seven hours. I

thought, "When the Lord is in charge, He knows when it's time to work fast."

"Cotton, when we get you home we need to check into a marble game—how about it?" I asked. I got the "Yep!" and smile from him again.

As we drove into Cotton's yard we saw his mother standing by the truck.

"Where have you been? I have been looking for you, young man," she asked.

I saw a look on her face that had never been there before. There was a true smile of relief for the first time in the few months we had known each other. She then walked to me and reached for my hand. Instead of shaking my hand, though she hugged me, with tears in her eyes.

She said, "Thanks to you, me and Cotton won't have to worry about getting cussed and fussed at no more."

I asked the mother how she was financially. Again I got another surprise. Cotton's mother said, "Before he opened the door for the sheriff he handed me his money and the stuff out of his pockets."

"How much did he have?" I asked.

She reached into the truck, got the bank bag and

handed it to me. I was surprised when I opened it. I saw many hundred-dollar bills.

I handed it back to her and said, "I won't ask where he got it; you will need it to take care of you and Cotton." I turned to my pal. "Mr. Cotton, are you ready for that marble game."

"Yep!" was the reply. He had a circle drawn and 13 marbles in a row across in it in no time at all.

While we were playing our marble game, and while I was getting beaten badly, I told Cotton what the man who lived with them said to me about his grandpa's shotgun.

I asked, "Cotton, that was your grandpa's shotgun and I know you loved him. Why did you hide it in the woods?"

I hoped he would talk to me about it and he said, "I hid it so I could get it and make him quit hurting my mama. And make them boys quit hurting me at school."

I asked him, "Will you show it to me when we get through with our game?"

"Yep!"

"Do you call it a game when you have blown off someone's doors?" I asked. "You have just knocked out 11 of the 13 marbles, I only have one and you are about to get the last one. What if I ask you not to tell anyone you beat me so bad—what would you say?"

"I won't tell nobody cause you ain't had no chance to practice since this morning." He smiled a wide smile as he knocked the last marble out. I remember thinking, and can tell you from experience, if this kid had been around when I was a kid he would have owned every kid's marble in our community if they played him for keeps.

He got up and with his foot erased the circle we had been playing in, smiled and said, "I wiped out the circle for good luck. If you want me to help you learn to shoot better, I will."

"I appreciate that, pal. You said you would show me your grandpa's shotgun."

"Yep! Come on and I will get it."

He went under the trailer and came out with a pillowcase and three dogs. The way they looked at me, if I had given only a hint of some kind of threat, I would have had big troubles. I thought at that time, "Those skinny dogs were under there all the time while we were playing marbles, watching for just the right time to give me a giant surprise."

Even to this day I get edgy thinking about what could have happened. I had not forgotten the time Cotton's mother ran them back under the trailer.

Cotton handed me the pillowcase and said, "Here is my grandpa's shotgun and shotgun shells."

I had not had the faintest idea it would be a shotgun that had been sawed off and the stock removed, with a towel wrapped around in its place.

"What is this?" I asked.

"A short skinny shotgun."

"Who cut it off and put the towel on it, and who put the string on it?"

Cotton answered, "I put the string on it and it was already cut off by my grandpa."

"Why the string," I asked.

"I thought I could put it around my neck and hide it under my shirt. So they couldn't see it."

"Who couldn't see it?" I asked.

"Him and them boys," Cotton said as calm as if he had thought it through many times and knew exactly what he was going to do.

"Boy, that is a bunch of shells," I said. "Cotton, have you ever shot your grandpa's shotgun?"

"Nope, but I saw grandpa shoot it a bunch of

times."

"Cotton, you must have felt pretty bad if you was thinking about hurting him and them boys with this shotgun, right?"

"Yep they wouldn't listen and always called me stinky and said I had lice, wouldn't let me use the bathroom and pushed my head in the commode and said I was a kid nobody liked, and said I must have had my hair cut by a chain saw."

I asked him what the boy's names were, and—surprise!—I knew all three of them. They had been in trouble for bullying other kids in their neighborhood. I knew I could deal with them harassing Cotton; they really weren't bad kids.

I told Cotton to ask his mother to come outside. When she saw the shotgun she recognized it instantly and asked several questions in one sentence, "Where did it come from? Cotton did you have it some place? Where did you have it? Why did you take it? Why did you want to hide your grandpa's old shotgun?"

When I told her what Cotton had told me, she put her hand over her mouth and started to cry. All she could say was, "What? What?"

"I will have to take this shotgun and shells with

me," I said. I told Cotton, "I'm proud of you, my boy, and I won't tell anyone you took the shotgun if you promise me you won't tell people how bad I did in our marble game. You want to promise?"

"Yep," he said sticking out his hand and said, "I'll shake on it and you know when someone shakes hands, they are buddies."

I shook his hand and said, "You are absolutely right, Cotton, old buddy."

"How about helping me take your bike out of my car. There is somewhere I want my new buddy to go with me, ok?" I said.

When he was in my car I told his mother that I was taking him to the Western Auto store to buy him a new bike. I don't know if she had taken her hand from her mouth since she had placed it there in surprise. With tears still in her eyes, she removed her hand slowly and waved and said, "OK."

On the way to town I asked myself, "What would have happened if Cotton had taken this shotgun to school?" Thank the Lord it didn't happen.

It was hard for the boy to make up his mind with so many bright colors. The next day everyone in Red Bud community saw a smiling Cotton on his canary
196

yellow bike, with several reflectors on the mud flaps and in the spokes of the wheels.

After a psychiatric evaluation and psychological counseling to help Cotton adjust and deal with the troubles he had been experiencing, Cotton's life began to make dramatic changes.

Just before Cotton and his mother moved back to North Carolina, I went with them to a teacher's conference. The teacher's comments were that Cotton was doing very well and was on grade level, had perfect attendance, had made the honor roll, was very cheerful, got along well with other classmates and that since they were moving she was recommending that he not be placed in special education at his new school.

I remember thinking a short prayer, "Thank you, Lord, for letting me see one of your miracles."

Cotton that day was a far cry from that skinny, pathetic, unkempt, undernourished, sad-eyed, unsmiling kid that I saw riding a bike with a lopsided wheel around Red Bud.

Thirty years later my images of him are frozen in time. Although most of Cotton's later story remains shrouded in mystery, his life did touch mine in a special way.

Thinking of him, I wonder about the love that is just under the surface of little troubled kids, and the courage it takes for them to trust, to rise above what hurts, to please, and to be one of the crowd.

I marvel at his mother's shy courage, simple honesty and thankfulness. She was a caring mother who got trapped in a no-win situation.

Most of all, even today I wonder about all those little lonely misfits—of which there are many—that walk the halls of our schools.

I also think about Columbine High School in Colorado and the other schools where students did horrible things to their classmates. I know someone saw those troubled kids, and if they had taken enough time maybe tragedies could have been averted.

When I occasionally visit Cotton's old haunts in Red Bud, I wish I could see him ride by, fishing rod, gunnysacks and all. I'd like to wave him over now, walk through Newt's neighborhood with him as two adults, and just talk... about everything.

And who knows, maybe shoot marbles. But not for keeps.

Spunkie Keener

I've already told you a little bit about my pal, Spunkie Keener. But I'd like to share a little more about Spunkie and how knowing him has been a blessing to me.

Regardless of who we are, we each have a unique gift to share with the world. Spunkie will never go to college, run for political office, or live on his own. But his gift is that he is truly colorblind and does not judge others based on their cultural heritage, educational or religious backgrounds, wealth, sexual preference, or mental or physical abilities.

Almost everyone he meets gets a smile and a hug. Perhaps the greatest lesson Spunkie has taught us is one of self-acceptance. Spunkie just is, take him or leave him.

As long as I live I will never forget the greatest lesson he ever taught me, when he showed me how to love someone the way our Maker meant for us to love others.

Spunkie mourned when Mama Balliew died, but he knew that Mama was in Heaven's House. Spunkie knew that that Heaven's House was right down the

201

road. He knew it because he learned it when Mama Balliew passed away. He knew that she had gone to a peaceful place where she could talk to Jesus.

Spunkie had learned that Jesus was a fisherman; Spunkie also figured out that Mama Balliew must have been talking to Jesus about him. "She must have told Jesus to help me catch a big fish," he said, "because Jesus helped me catch a 5 ½ pound bass on a little bitty hook."

He quite often looks at his bass that is hanging displayed on his bedroom wall, that Mrs. Balliew and Jesus helped him catch.

Spunkie was a handful when he first came to live with us. He was 8 years old yet still in diapers. He could not talk, bit his own arms, had large sores on his elbows and head from hitting them on the floors and walls, had very poor hygiene and was unable to attend school, because those in the county could not handle him or keep him from hurting other children.

His was one of the most extreme cases of autism ever seen in this area. Our Gordon County Special Education Department helped him to get into another school outside the county that was essential to prepare him to be able to attend our schools.

202

Once he began attending school, Spunkie would beat himself unmercifully with objects and each day when he exited his school bus he would began hitting himself with his book bag.

At that time Michelle became a special person in Spunkie's life. She began to understand his scrambled words, eventually learning that Spunkie was being teased at school—one of the main reasons for his self-abuse.

Michelle convinced Spunkie that the other children were joking with him only because they liked him and thought he was a super kid. Her love and understanding changed his way of seeing things, and Spunkie began to grow in ways that nobody had ever dreamed.

Spunkie is a blessing every day, but on one special day, he touched the lives of many. On that day we traveled to our local Seventh-day Adventist Church to say goodbye to Michelle. She was set to depart for Haiti, in hopes of giving some of that country's troubled children a brighter future. All Spunkie knew was that she was leaving.

In the parking lot, Spunkie walked slowly up to Michelle and gave her the biggest hug anyone has ever given. Then he turned, bowed his head and ambled away. I noticed that Spunkie was shaking and with his epilepsy I immediately thought he was having a seizure, but upon closer inspection, found that he was sobbing.

Spunkie has only shed tears on two occasions, when Mrs. Balliew died and that day, when he hugged Michelle goodbye. As we comforted him, we asked him about his feelings.

Spunkie replied, "Mrs. Balliew go to Heaven House, she not come home no more. Michelle going to Haiti's house. She not coming home, she not coming back to my home no more."

In his mind, he thought of Haiti and Heaven as the same place. In these simple words, Spunkie conveyed the love he had for Michelle and the deep sorrow he felt that she was leaving. With his words and tears, he showed that he understood that a greater joy exists in Heaven.

Regardless of how much Spunkie loved Michelle, he was willing to let her go and experience the magnificence that waited just down the road at Heaven's House.

How many people can ever expect to have such a devoted friend as Spunkie? Spunkie is a living example of a true friend and I am thankful he calls me his buddy.

The Winners Club

From the book TAPE IT TO YOUR HEART by Tony
Reynolds, a Winners Club alumnus

The Winners Club is a place of dreams and big-time love. The club was founded in 1971 by Deacon Balliew to assist children who face personal, physical, mental and behavioral challenges.

Deacon started serving his community as a juvenile probation officer in Calhoun, Georgia. He saw firsthand the direction that many children were heading. To meet the need, Deacon started a Scout troop for mentally challenged boys. After a few years, the organization expanded to include girls and adults and became known as The Winners Club. At the age of five, because I had three brothers who were members, the opportunity was also extended to me. After five years, I became one of the leaders. Today, I am praising Deacon for his commitment to his community. To help you get a better understanding of this man, I'm going to share a few stories with you. Singing for President Jimmy Carter at the age of six didn't even make my list of top 20.

In 1988, Deacon and a six-year old-child were at the local hardware store in Calhoun. A man said to Deacon, "I think it is great how you are taking care of those people. If there is any way that I can assist you, please just let me know."

The man looked down at the child, then back at Deacon, and said, "Do you know that there is a colored boy following you?" Deacon reached down, picked the boy up, gave him a big hug, and said, "I see nobody of color. All I see is my son." Twenty-five years later, he still calls me his son.

Michael was 12 when he started going to the club, and we soon learned he had a brain tumor. One day Deacon asked the boy if he ever had a dream. "I've never seen the ocean," he said. Not too long afterward, Michael's doctor told his mother that he didn't have much time to live. Michael's mother called Deacon and informed him of the situation. By the time she had driven home from the doctor's office, Deacon had lined up an airplane, a pilot, a deep-sea charter boat, a hotel, and Michael's doctor to be available by phone in case he was needed. Several weeks later, Michael passed away. Prior to his passing, he told his mother that he was ready to go because Deacon allowed him to see what heaven was going to be like.

When I was in the 9th grade, my first day of varsity football practice, I was run over time and time again. I got hurt, but it was mostly my pride that ached. Even though we only had 27 players, I thought I was going to get cut from the team, and they never cut anyone. I heard a teammate say, "If I was Tony, I would quit." I never understood why I didn't quit. It wasn't because he had made me so mad that I wasn't going to let him get the best of me. Several years later, I knew the reason. Deacon taught me that I was a winner, and winners never quit.

Then and now, Deacon accepts everyone who crosses his path with unconditional love. He tries to teach everyone what it means to be a winner.

- You are not a winner because you came in first place.
- You are not a winner because you won the biggest trophy.
- You are not a winner because you picked the right number.
- You are a winner because you didn't quit and you finished the race.

Last week as I talked to Deacon on the phone, I

could hear and feel the love in every word he spoke to me. We began to discuss the things that God had done with our lives. He asked me if I remembered the first conversation we ever had when I told him that I wanted to be a member of the Winners Club. It was funny, because I did. "You asked me what I was going to say if my friends start picking on me for being in the Winners Club and for being friends with a white man." I was five at the time and I said my answer would be, "Deacon is my father. You may look at us and say that is impossible. I look at us and I see no difference. I see a man who loves my family and me for who and what we are. I see a man who showed me what it meant to be a winner. The members of the Winners Club are my brothers and sisters."

When I think of who has had the greatest impact on my life, besides God and my family, I think of Deacon. Deacon still lives in Calhoun, has advanced his work to show the disadvantaged in Haiti what it means to be a winner, and still says, "God made all of us, and He doesn't make any mistakes, and this is for certain, we can all be winners at something."

A Most Unforgettable Character

In the past 30 years I've had the opportunity to cross paths with many unforgettable and notable people who have shown caring and devotion to the handicapped young people I was associated with.

The one that I can't get off my mind at the present is Eunice Kennedy Shriver. In the 1950s and 1960s most of the mentally retarded were hidden or kept out of sight. I can remember those times very vividly.

It was in the late 1960s. We had begun a Boy Scout troop for mentally retarded fellows and a Girl Scout troop for the young ladies in Gordon County.

I remember the exact words to a prayer I said that seemed so simple at that time, but today it seems the most important prayer I know the Lord answered when I said, "Please help me Lord. I know I'm going to need a bunch of your help with this situation I've gotten myself in, Amen"

Mrs. Shriver in those troubling years had been very successful in getting her family to go public with her sister Rose Mary's difficulty of being retarded and having to be placed out of the family.

I remember asking how she persuaded her family to do what I knew was very hard for them.

"I had lots of help," she said. "You should know. Look at what you are doing."

I wish now I had asked who other than God was the most help. I know one thing for sure she had a gleam in her eyes when she talked about those times. Who would ever believe that Americans with a disabled person in their families would benefit so much from that lady's dream?

In 1968, mainly through her efforts, Special Olympics Inc. was established to help the mentally retarded. That historic trail since then has been a fantastic one of love and caring that has involved millions of volunteers and mentally challenged people around the world.

That trail in 1970 I began to walk and helped me really realize that I would be working with troubled young people for the rest of my life. And that was the time I remembered my prayer of a year or so back.

"Please help me Lord I know I'm going to need a bunch of your help with this situation I got myself in, Amen."

Our Gordon County group of athletes had been

invited to the first ever Georgia State Special Olympic finals in Decatur.

I was standing on the track talking with Tommy Nobis who at the time was a very talented linebacker with the Atlanta Falcons and one of the founders of Georgia Special Olympics.

We were having a good time chatting with one of our athletes, Mike Casey, when from behind us our Georgia. Special Olympic state director said, "Mrs. Shriver, this is Deacon Balliew, our Northwest Georgia director from Gordon County."

Mrs. Shriver said, "And this is the Deacon from North Georgia I've been hearing about."

In shocked surprise I think I said, "Yes ma'am, " without thinking to put out my hand to shake until she almost had to reach for mine.

She told me how much she appreciated what we were doing up here and would be seeing me later. Mrs. Shriver as she turned to walk away said, "I hear you are also a Scoutmaster for a Boy Scout troop of young men with mental retardation. I want you to know your guys are one of the first Boy Scout troops I've heard about."

I didn't know at the time we were one of the first Boy Scout troops for the retarded in the nation. Later

211

that evening I had a few minutes to discuss the Scout troop and what we were doing, and an acquaintance with Mrs. Shriver developed.

I had the opportunity to see Mrs. Shriver on other occasions and was surprised to find out that she had worked for the juvenile court system. At the time I was working for the Gordon County Juvenile Court and was amazed at her knowledge and ideas on juvenile matters.

On one particular occasion we were sitting in the bleachers in Athens talking about our work with the retarded when she looked me straight in the eyes and said, "Deacon, I have no doubt you will understand what I'm going to tell you. It's what a priest once said, and I'd like to share with you. Deacon, can you remember seeing a mentally retarded young person accomplish something that amazed you and all the others around him, and none of you could understand how it happened?"

I looked out on the track at our group of athletes and thought about Mike Casey and his birdies on the golf course and the deer he killed with a bow and arrow, Adel Keener with our group singing "Amazing Grace" for President Jimmy Carter, and most of all the Tanner brothers, Tony and Duane, and the fantastic personal change they had made in their lives in such a short time and how those two mustered the courage and trust to try new things had astonished everyone.

I then answered, "Yes ma'am, I've seen things like that happen several times."

I can see her face as if we were sitting together at this moment. I have tried to remember exactly what she said and the way she said it because it has helped me when I was down, depressed, and worried—a beacon of hope to keep focused on ever since.

In a matter of a few seconds and I'm not sure it's word for word or each word being the same she said to me, "Deacon the Lord had permitted you to see Him creating His miracles and once He permitted you to see Him doing that He had chosen you because you have been faithful to your mission He had placed you on. And He will permit and bless you with many more opportunities to see things happen that no one could explain.

"The community will say it is amazing what those people are doing. I can't believe it, it must be a miracle. Always remembering it's the Lord's doing His work. Many times people will not understand your reasoning or decisions and that's when the devil and his advocates will create confusion and heartaches at every turn if you permit them. He could be wearing a very familiar face or faces you thought were friends but turned out to be only acquaintances.

"And keep in mind The Lord will also, when asked, let you know when He has other missions for you to follow. I believe when you or your missions begin to be judged by people without knowledge of His work, He is preparing you to make decisions about things only you will understand. Don't ever forget God's love will be near always and He will always hear when asked to help." I remember during that
214

discussion she referred to Mother Mary several times.

She then talked about experiences and how she had dealt with them, which I have never forgotten.

Over the years I sure know now all about the devil and his advocates and have always tried to be prepared. It's amazing what prayer will do for a situation when the devil's crowd is around.

I have never forgotten her telling me those things so honestly, hoping I could remember how to explain it so people would understand and I have thanked the Lord many times for blessing me with the chance to see him created His miracles.

While Mrs. Shriver was telling me that, there was a look in her eyes and on her face that I will never forget. A saintly look I guess, especially when she said the words "miracle and Mother Mary." One thing for sure, I had no doubt she was a very religious lady and knew what she was talking about. I also knew for certain if she had not been in those types of situation and experienced God's love she couldn't have given such sound advice.

The last time I saw her in person, she was standing with a group of coaches discussing a sad story of an elderly lady and her Down's syndrome son who could not talk. I knew the lady and the situation they were discussing. I knew her and her son from Special Olympic track meets in Dalton.

I can remember how impressed I was at how she interpreted for him and how happy the two were; there were times they laughed together that were infectious. Without knowing it we were all smiling or laughing with them.

My family also knew her and her family who lived in another city. We had heard that she had been diagnosed with terminal cancer with only a few months to live. We were told she had tried unsuccessfully to find relatives or friends to help her locate a place for her son when she wouldn't be able to care for him any longer.

The young man was non-verbal and only she could understand his verbal sounds, hand motions, and gestures. She found there was no family or friends who would be able to care for him when he would need them. The only place that she could find for him to live when she would not be here for him any longer, was far away from all family in a special needs home, and she became very depressed.

I will never forget the evening we received the

phone call. The caller told us she left a note, which if I remember correctly simply said, "I know I love him and want him and the only other one that I know loves him and wants him is Jesus so I am going to take him with me to be with Jesus," and signed her name. That lady then took that young man's life and her own.

I didn't tell that group of coaches that I knew of them and how sad the situation really was, just that I knew the young man was a Special Olympian. I have over the years heard of families with special needs children worrying about their child's future when they will need someone to help.

That was over 18 years ago, and our family had just gotten custody of an 8-year-old mentally retarded young fellow by the name of Spunkie Keener who was a bundle of super hyperactive mischief and a little clown.

We were standing close to Mrs. Shriver's table discussing how we had gotten custody of Spunkie and the reasoning behind it. She spoke of a couple who several years before had gotten custody of a retarded child and was almost immediately faced with making life-changing decisions because of the child and his needs.

217

She said, "I know your family put much thought and prayer into your decision, and I can tell everyone really loves that young man."

I don't remember our family thinking about any life- changing thoughts at that time, but there was not a doubt about us loving him. How can you not love a little fellow who lets you know with all his existence that he loves you?

She then patted me on the hand and said, "May God bless and guide you and your family when those life-altering times comes. Remembering that boy is one of his children. Very few people will understand and many times only people with a special needs child and very close friends will know what you are experiencing. You at times will be criticized for decisions you have to make. And those will be very trying and lonesome times. When people start judging the love you have for someone, always remember that the Almighty will understand and guide you. And in the end He will be the only one you will have to answer to."

Never have I heard a truer statement. Unless you have seen or experienced those times, you cannot fully appreciate or understand.

We, like the lady with the Down's Syndrome son,

understand and are concerned about Spunkie's future. Spunkie has a severe speech impediment and only our family understands most of his unintelligible scrambled words and their meanings. I can remember his misty eyes and how frustrated he would become when he tried to communicate with people.

His life and his world began to change drastically when we started to understand and make sense out of what he was saying. He went from the frustrated, angry hurting young fellow that had to be physically restrained by his teachers to keep him from hurting them, himself or the other children to a kid that received The Jeff Townsend Attendance Award for 13 years perfect school attendance and received a Special Education Diploma from Gordon Central High School.

And today he attends The George Chambers Resource Center with a few of his lifelong buddies. There he is learning important survival skills that will help him for the rest of his life.

We now know love, patience, and many prayers will help God create one of his miracles. Spunkie Keener is living proof.

What would happen to Spunkie if he didn't have

or feel the security of a family? Like the lady and her son we mentioned earlier we hadn't thought that much about his future, and it began to worry us.

One of the things most people can understand and needs is the security of a family. Spunkie is our proof of it. Our family has tried to make our home a permanent refuge from the things he worries about. We are committed as a family in assuring him he will always have that security, and always have the feeling of being loved and cared for.

I know he still remembers and gets scared when reminded of his distant past, and we know he worries about the future. There are times he gets so close to me he physically presses against me; there are times he will actually grasp my clothing or hand to keep me from getting too far away when situations scare, worry, or confuse him.

We all know love is a gift from God, and we each respond to the feeling in our own way. We sometimes are surprised and don't appreciate how God will open our eyes to the love we have for each other until we are confronted with a situation that makes us realize it.

Our family did and made another of those life-altering decisions Mrs. Shriver talked about. We have noticed how relaxed and contented Spunkie has been lately when talking about his family.

Mrs. Shriver was like a saint, and I have always remembered her advice and the statement "There will be times no one will understand except your closest friends, families in your situation and the Lord when you have to make those life-changing decisions. And in the end he is the only one you will have to answer to."

Our family recently made one of those decisions, and she was also right about people not understanding.

I feel I have neglected Spunkie, my family, and my loved ones. I had let the Winners Club become an obsession, my life, not my job, not my calling, like the head of a 50-member family that I feel had caused me to become very narrow-focused, just like I was in a barrel.

I have gotten to where I could see very little outside the barrel. Inside that barrel was the Winners Club and its responsibilities, the little fellows with all their and their families' problems, doing individual, group, and family counseling, and family therapy all on a continuing basis, upkeep of the building and grounds, raising funds to operate, planning most of activities, being up at 5 a.m. and stopping at 9 p.m. or later then transferring the phone to our house, maintaining all the vehicles, driving hundreds of miles weekly transporting our young fellows to and from our weekly meetings and their families to doctors all over the state, and to other places when a ride was needed, attending along with parents all meetings at schools when required for the children, taking some of our kids to church most Sundays, working with volunteers, having our home available on many occasions for the children to stay before a trip, as a reward for a job well done or when their families were in conflict, just to list a few of the Winners Club duties, not to mention all those other things I was volunteered to do in the community.

That vision has controlled and dictated what I did with my life for the past three decades, and the future was looking the same.

I have slowed down now and asked the Lord to help me redefine my priorities and His mission he has had me on. It has now been 37 years and 630 troubled young people and all their varied problems.

We have never had a vacation or visited our families without some of our kids being with us, always planning trips for the kids on our off days and holidays. We've never planned a weekend trip without thinking how we can involve the kids, always transferring our phone to all those distant locations just in case one of the kids or families had a problem and needed our assistance.

I plan now with the Lord's help to start looking outside of that barrel and redirect my time and energy in ways I have neglected in the past, which I feel are many.

I know I will need His help in adjusting to the changes. I know I will forever love and never forget any of those hundreds of smiling faces. I'll ever be thankful for the Lord having permitted me to become part of their families, to share with them their sadness, worries, frustrations, tears, failures, happinesses, successes and God's Love.

And in many cases years later having their little ones hug my neck. A much less troubled child than their parents were.

I feel like they are my grandchildren. I know I sure feel like their grandpa.

But as Mrs. Shriver said, "If you are faithful to His mission He placed you on; you will see many of His miracles." She was one of the most intelligent and caring individuals who gave me advice so many years ago. Advice I'm recalling and using still today.

She must have been able to predict the future. Or at least our family now thinks so. "You will know when there are other missions he has for you to follow."

The Winners Club was the mission I have no doubt He placed me on. It has taken many prayers asking Him to show me and help me understand his priorities, which now have become mine.

After all, these 37 years were His idea in the first place. I am a truly blessed man and have thanked God many times for His love and patience and allowing me to be present when He created His miracles.

Deep down I know these two things and have tried to live by them: What matters in this life is not winning ourselves. What matters in this life is helping others to win even if it means slowing down and changing our course.

And I thank God for always reminding me if we can wipe away from any child's cheek a tear, then we will not have lived in vain while here.

I will be retiring as the executive director of the Winners Club at the end of this year.

Our Board of Directors search committee has been actively taking applications in search of a new executive director. They know and understand what the mission of the Winners Club has been for the past 37 years.

Our mission is to give a child a place to develop hope where little existed, and always must be to help handicapped children and their families accomplish their dreams. Our community has always supported our organization in fantastic ways because of those kids and their families' success and the love that the Winners Club has generated in our community.

I know the community will continue to support this organization because it is going to keep the same focus.

Upon retiring Dec. 31, 2003 I will begin my new mission as coordinator of the Preschool of Handicapped Children in Roi, Haiti, that a group in Calhoun recently organized.

I'm excited about our community giving those little fellows down there, hope and something to dream about.

Many children in Haiti—like many of the physically and mentally handicapped children we have been blessed to see and help in the Winners Club over the years—will actually die before they reach the age of

6 or 7 from malnutrition, or as I had it explained to me by a missionary from Haiti the other day, they will starve to death.

I've also made Spunkie a promise; I am going to be spending a lot of time with him and his buddies which are also my oldest and dearest friends. They are the Scout group that led to the existence of the Winners Club.

I am excited about having a lot of fun with those fellows again. I know Mrs. Shriver would agree with my new mission. I think all can certainly see why Mrs. Eunice Kennedy Shriver is one of my most unforgettable characters.

I am going to start looking for ways to tell our community what it has accomplished with its love and support, how with so much caring and understanding it has on many occasions absolutely changed the lives forever of little children and their families.

How on so many occasions it has broken the molds and forever changed the destiny of future generations.

My prayer has changed very little over the years: "Thank you Father for your LOVE, what you have given me the opportunity to see, my family and please

226

help me Lord I know I'm going to need a bunch of your help with this situation I have gotten myself in, Amen."

Heroes Find How to Pick Up the Pieces

From the beginning of time, there have been individuals who have accomplished great deeds, known as heroes. I am not referring to heroes who wear capes and masks. I am not referring to the tall, dark and handsome men, or the tall, blond, blue-eyed women that Hollywood showed us as the ideal heroes. The dictionary defines a hero as "a person distinguished for exceptional courage, fortitude, or bold enterprise. One idolized for superior qualities or deeds of any kind." A hero is a person who is known for standing their ground.

Heroes are the people who can pick up the pieces, reassemble them in some kind of working order, doing it as if they were destined for that purpose and then stand their ground. You will find being able to stand their ground is the common factor in heroes.

I often think of these people as my heroes. Heroes I would like to sit with and talk, and ask them to explain the tough times and what it took to stand their ground.

My ultimate hero is Jesus Christ. He stood his ground and persevered even as he faced death. He became the role model, setting the example for all heroes thereafter with his determination, bravery, valor, fortitude, conviction, loyalty, courage, and dedication. He was focused, selfless and willing to sacrifice himself with a humble heart, loving soul, and an unselfish mind. It is my belief no one person can ever expect to, or will, possess all these qualities as Christ did.

Chief Joseph of the Wallowa Band of the Nez Perce Indians, who said after he and his people were forced by the US Government to leave their homes, and live on a reservation, "The earth is Mother of all people and all people should have equal rights upon it." After being lied to so many times by our government and its treaties while trying to defend his people's rights, he knew his people would all be killed if they continued to resist. So he said, "From where the sun now stands, I shall fight no more, forever." He saved the lives of his people, but died later, some say of a broken heart.

Heroism is not reserved for men only. There are acts of heroism accomplished by children and women. There is a powerful force that drives many of us to

230

deeds that takes great courage.

Miss Helen Keller altered our perception of the disabled and remapped the boundaries of sight and sense. She did this while being deaf, blind and nonverbal as a child. She was a remarkable lady.

All true heroes are champions. They clearly saw where the pieces were in disarray and tried to put them back together in some kind of order. For some reason they were able to preserve trust that was placed in them.

I want to tell you about some young people who are heroes and champions to me, and to the people whose lives they affected.

As you know, I worked with the Juvenile Court for a time, and while there I met a hero—I called him Little Man. I remember the courage it took you to stop me in the breezeway of Calhoun Elementary School. He said he was afraid to talk to me there because the gang of bullies would beat him up if they knew he was telling me about them, so we met later.

He told me about the group who was bullying him and other kids at school, and harassing people in the housing projects on the west side of Calhoun. These young bullies were organized with the intent of causing fear in other young people and the elderly. He told me about an elderly lady who had been giving them money because they had threatened to harm her.

With his courage, we were able to break up that gang of bullies that was terrorizing the neighborhood. Little Man is a true hero. He took the challenge, and with courage, stood his ground. Together we were able to put the pieces back in good order again.

Blondie is also one of my heroes. I remember when she told me about the drugs, alcohol and violence in her family. She told me about beatings her mother was enduring, the whippings she received and how many nights she never slept because of fear.

Blondie ran away from home on several occasions. I will never forget how nervous she was and how she cried while discussing her fears. Blondie's courage is the reason her family finally began to truly be a family and continues successfully today. It is humbling how every time we see each other she tells me she still loves me. I love you, too, young lady.

It was her courage that kept us friends all these years. She is my hero because of her selfless fortitude, and for standing her ground while helping to put the pieces of her family back together again. Her two children are about as close as my own grandchildren.

I am proud of her. She broke the mold, and her future generations will forever be different. She stayed focused, showed outstanding perseverance, unbelievable sacrifice and had the courage to ask for help.

For the rest of my life, I will never forget the courage and the caring that Rabbit felt for her brothers and sisters. I can still hear her trembling, stuttering voice on the phone when she was telling me she was afraid for the safety of her brothers and sisters and herself.

When I asked how she knew to call me, she said, "When my brother came to your office when he was in trouble, you told him to call you if he was worried or scared, and you would help him. You gave him a card with your name on it, and he put it in his drawer. I got it out, climbed out of the window, and came over here to the neighbor's house to call you."

Rabbit told me why she was afraid. After I told her to stay where she was, I looked at my watch and saw it was almost midnight. The Sheriffs Department responded to my phone call for another officer to meet me near her home. On the way there I remembered seeing all of Rabbit's brothers and sisters in the courthouse hallway with their mother. I knew she couldn't have been more than ten or twelve years old, and that she had four or five brothers and sisters.

After talking to Rabbit at her neighbors, I went to her home and found her two little brothers and two sisters locked in the bedroom. She told me her parents were drunk, and they were.

But she didn't tell me they were cleaning pieces of machinery in a dishpan of gasoline near the fireplace with a log fire. She didn't mention that the house was in such a terrible condition; there was mildewed food on shelves and piles of smelly garbage in the corners. She didn't mention that all the kids were in one bedroom without a source of heat—a bedroom that smelled terrible because some of them had to use one corner as a bathroom.

I remember holding her baby brother, who had her little pink rabbit, in my arms. The rest of the little guys were holding onto my arm and the officer's hands as we talked with their grandmothers. Rabbit's parents were being taken to jail.

I will never forget the comment she made on the way to her grandmothers: "Deacon Balliew, I'm scared for my mother going to jail."

She was just eleven years old. The courage it took to make that call was what put her family on its path to where they are today. She is my hero, and she is beautiful.

Rabbit is a teacher now, and I see how she shows the students in her classroom how if feels to be loved. I know she expects them to be the best they can be. We both know loving them is the key. We also both know that you may be the only one who shows them any love at all.

A lot of naysayer family members predicted doom and gloom about where Rabbit and her sister and brothers were going to wind up. Man, did they ever miss the mark! I have to say all of those kids are heroes.

I want to stop here and talk about the naysayers and how they affect children's lives. We've all met those guys. They are not heroes in many people's books, but how in the world would we get along without them? Naysayers are the masters of doom and gloom. For some unknown reason, they think they have been given the gift to predict the future. Since the beginning of time they have been around, but it seems to me they should have learned from their ancestors, that they don't have a clue about predicting the future.

The dictionary describes a naysayer as someone who has the tendency to take a gloomy view of affairs or situations and to anticipate the worst. Some of the synonyms used to describe those guys are *pessimist*, *worry wart* and *wet blanket*. They have no place in a child's life.

I can hear them now, "What is the world coming to? The way this kid is acting he will never amount to anything; the way this younger generation is acting the world will have to be ending soon." Our grandparents heard that prediction—we all have. I predict the naysayers will continue to miss the mark with their predictions. When I hear one of them start in, I tell them, "Man, don't even go there with me. I believe the Lord said he would make the decision when the world would be finished, not any of us."

I've sort of strayed from the subject; I get on the defensive when I hear our younger generation criticized. The young people I have worked with have heard it a lot.

We also need to realize: when our young people become adults, they will possess the ethics, values, and morals we all are living in front of and teaching them.

We are the living examples. What they become in the future depends a lot on us adults.

I think in spite of us, the adults, the world is going to be okay. I especially feel this way when I think of some of our younger heroes. This younger generation is our future and I feel pretty good about it.

There's another group of local heroes that really got my attention a few years ago. Like I stated before, I believe a hero is a person who, above all odds, can take on a challenge, stand their ground, and put things into some kind of working order.

The heroes I have been describing are not necessarily the same as a sports champion hero who wins a competition and is temporarily ranked "Number One." I always tried to teach children to understand that to be a champion or someone's hero, they needed to be strong willed, focused, selfless and determined.

They needed to be able to set their minds to achieve a goal or solve a problem, and stand their ground while doing their best. When they learned to do so, they would begin to feel confident and proud. They would become respected and everyone would see them as a worthy person that may be considered a champion, or maybe someone's hero.

I have told young people what makes a hero a hero, is that they accept a challenge and overcome risks in a manner that requires courage and sacrifice, and in some way benefits the community.

This may be over-simplified, but it's the heart of what a hero is to me. I have been blessed to be around many who took on a challenge and became heroes.

I again checked Mr. Webster's dictionary for his definitions and synonyms. This time, he hit the nail on the head. These young people did heroic acts, making them bold, courageous, fearless, gallant, brave and determined. It was like he knew I was going to tell you about these fellows. In a few minutes, you will agree with me. Every one of them fits his definition of a hero.

The heroes I am going to tell you about were teenagers who came to us early in their lives for help with conquering their personal problems. Over a period of a few years, through many tears and personal struggles, they and their families gradually succeeded, and become my life long friends.

It amazed me how they learned ways to get up each and every time they were knocked down. I watched them learn that they might fail, and winning was not the only thing. But they never quit. My pride in them grew even stronger when I noticed they were learning to do what was right, even when it hurt them.

I noticed that, during their struggles, our heroes began to lay aside many of their desires for the benefit of others. By devoting countless hours, they made dreams come true for a small group of champions that came to us for help.

Our group had a little champion in braces, who had heard people tell her she would probably be in a wheelchair for the rest of her life. She not only left the wheelchair to use a walker, but she began to take steps without her walker. Her dream was to walk into school like all the other children, not in a wheelchair.

She was very shy, and had very low self-esteem. She was going to a center for the mentally challenged, but dreamed of going to a regular school. With the youthful enthusiasm and devotion of our heroes and their help, her dream became a reality.

A large part of her success can be attributed to our young heroes, who were her role models. They gave her encouragement and never let her forget the dream. Every place she went, one or two of our heroes held her hand while she walked. Our teenaged heroes were learning to make things around them better and to do what was right, even when no one was watching. I remember thinking how much we loved each other and how close we had become.

Another synonym for hero is "champion," a person who shows exceptional fortitude, defends or fights for a person, belief, right or principle. Those teenagers were then, and still are, champions of the disabled.

A six-year-old boy in the group was mentally challenged and undeveloped, with cerebral palsy, braces, epilepsy, a hearing deficiency, allergies and social problems. I doubt this young fellow even knew how to dream or imagine what his future could hold.

Despite psychological tests labeling him a candidate for a class for the mentally and physically challenged, I saw him go from a shy, withdrawn little guy with all his challenges to a boy with hearing aids, his seizures under control and placement in a public school. He did all this in less than one year.

I strongly believe that if our young heroes hadn't spent all those one-on-one hours teaching him his alphabet, numbers, colors and shapes, and all the hours of physical activities to improve his coordination and attention, he would not have been able to register in a regular school that year.

He entered school a smiling, self-confident little fellow that was not afraid or ashamed to say "Thank you" or "I love you." These are words he learned to say because he heard them from our young heroes.

These are only two stories of lives our teenaged heroes touched. There were a dozen more. These guys and gals are still my heroes and we still know, love and see each other quite often.

As you can see, our community is a much better

place because those teenaged heroes took time to care.

There are countless young heroes in our communities, who are quietly doing things that make them champions and heroes. I have been blessed with the opportunity to see many of them do heroic acts.

I feel we as a society only look at adults as heroes, and as usual, we got it wrong again. We all need to look at the definition of a hero again, and apply the title where it belongs. I suppose my being involved with young people all my life will cause me to be a bit prejudiced.

But because I've been a volunteer and around adult volunteers most of my life, I think it may not be prejudiced thinking, but fact. Our young people are fantastic when it comes to caring.

The best measure of any society is how well it takes care of its weakest and most vulnerable members. Not how it caters and cares for it's strongest and most powerful citizens. It is obviously heartless and wrong when a society chooses to not take care of its weakest, its most needy and its most vulnerable citizens. Many volunteer organizations that care for physically and mentally challenged youth and adults are quietly shifting their focus away, when they should be getting

242

more focused.

I can assure you our youngest citizens as a whole are as caring and understanding as we adults. If you will slow down and take time to notice, you will also agree. Almost all our young people have the heart, and if given the chance, will be champions and heroes.

I hear the naysayers speaking now of how bad things are getting. Well, this fellow begs to differ with all of them. I think we are going to be just fine. We have a fantastic group of future leaders. I see them every time I enter our schools and churches. I guess you can see by now my favorite heroes are your kids, your young people.

I appreciate the jobs you parents are doing. I also know it is a struggle. We are going to be all right, thanks to your patience, and the examples you are setting.

There has to be some kind of powerful force that drives many of us to perform deeds that people to think are heroic acts. Thinking of those young heroes, I begin to wonder what it took to motivate them to serve their fellow man with such devotion.

It was, I believe, unselfishness and pure love that seemed to be their driving force. It gave them the will and strength to serve and love. Rest assured, the making of a hero does not require blue eyes, blond hair, being handsome, or ideal physical features.

What it required of those young people was someone willing to sacrifice, with a humble heart, a loving soul and with an unselfish mind—some of the same qualities possessed by my ultimate hero, Jesus.

Deacon of Hope

by Lee Walburn

No one preached a sermon there that Sunday in the Belmont Baptist Church. Not a sermon in the sense of scripture and exhortation and reminders of weakness of the flesh. Deacon Balliew, a sandy-haired man with hearing aids in ears traumatized by too many years of playing loud rock music, simply said to the congregation that he was proud to present the choir from The Winners Club, and the songs they sang that day began to crash against the heart like sunrise and flowers and rainbows.

The singers had come to Deacon Balliew as children. Not all were children in years, but almost all were childlike in terms of their minds. They were brought to him after most of society's institutions had been unable to unlock the windows of their minds and emotions. Many of them arrived with personal histories so tragic that the mouth dries out in the hearing of them.

Charlie Walker was a child then, and he will remain in that state of innocence of life. After the wreck on the highway, the one that had damaged

Charlie in ways doctors couldn't repair-though they did manage to bring him back four times from some place beyond sensate reality-his retentive memory was damaged. Whether it was through saving grace or cosmic irony, Charlie was left with the gift of music, glorious music that over the years has filled record albums.

Shane Pelfrey, tiny and fragile, was dressed in a candy-striped shirt and bright red tie on that Sunday. He sat in his wheelchair beside the pulpit, sat motionless except for his head, which moved slowly in time to the rapturous hymn "Peace in the Valley," and a lock of hair tumbled over his forehead, his eyes heavy with emotion. A shaft of light knifing through a window fell across the boy in the way morning light through church windows sometimes creates moments of illusion. I leaned across the pew and whispered to my friend Frank Spence, who had brought me there, "Am I crazy, or is that an angel sitting on that kid's shoulder?"

"Yeah," Frank said. "I've seen him there before."

Nevertheless, if this were just a story of rhapsodic illusion in a sliver of time, if this were just

246

the story of a man who taught mentally and physically disadvantaged children to sing, the story of 69-year-old William "Deacon" Balliew would not have matured into legend, would not have brought him honors from the state House to the White House. There would have been no reason last week to drive to Calhoun, to sit in the rocker on his front porch and listen to the stories again and finally to hear how the evil of life can temporarily extinguish the flame of even the brightest candle.

This is the way it all started. Deacon had settled in Calhoun to work in a carpet mill after post rock 'n' roll training as a bowling alley mechanic failed to brighten his horizon and that of his wife, Inez, and their two boys. He began to coach the youngest of the town's athletes, and from the start he had a special way with special children-those who were shy, uncoordinated or weak. In 1968, a friend asked him if he would take a few retarded children camping. Euphemisms like mentally challenged had not been developed at the time.

That was the start of the Boy Scout troop that would become momentarily famous. He discovered that one boy could tie knots faster than anybody else.

247

Another could build the best campfire. When they joined together in tug of war, they found the sum of their strength equaled anyone else's. They competed in Scout camporees. In fact, they earned so many merit badges that they were recognized as one of the best Scout troops in America. President Jimmy Carter brought them to the White House.

From that seed, nurtured first in an old storage shed, grew The Winners Club, as did Deacon's epiphany and conviction that "God doesn't make mistakes," that everyone can be a winner at something. Over the years, more than 600 of life's castaways achieved things nobody else thought they could do because of physical and mental disadvantage or as victims of life's cruelest traumas.

Example: The 8-year-old boy who was brought to the club in diapers, who had to be tied to a chair in school to keep him form hurting himself or others, who came to live with Deacon and Inez, whose speech impediment inspired long periods of sullen silence, who looked up one day and said clearly, "I love you, Mr. Balliew."

One of his girls did a command performance, for President Jimmy Carter singing 'Amazing Grace.'

248

Another is working toward a doctorate. Eight members have graduated from college. One received a football scholarship to the State University of West Georgia and made the Dean's list. One simply rose from the ashes of physical limitation to play just enough minutes to earn the precious football letter at Calhoun High. Countless others learned to refinish furniture, grow gardens, can vegetables, cook and bake and sew. Most learned to love themselves.

Example: There came to Deacon a shy boy with hair so thick and swirling he was called "Curly." His real name was Jackie Proctor, and he could do one thing: he could run. He could run so fast wind had to chase him. But he could not run for Calhoun High because his capacity for learning prevented his admission to the school's track team. Deacon Balliew made Jackie Proctor a promise. Someday everyone in town would know of his great gift of speed.

For three years, two and three times a week, Deacon took the boy to the high school track to train in solitude. Word began to spread about the boy who could run. People began to show up just to see him race the wind. Then one day he stopped racing the wind and began to race against other special people.

249

Nobody locally, nobody in the state, nobody in the region could beat him. Soon, everyone wondered if anyone in the world could beat him. At Brockport, New York, in the International Special Olympics, nobody could. Jackie Proctor beat the record for the 200 meters that for years was not equaled by anyone at the high school whose team he could not run for.

Jackie Proctor threw away his running shoes after the race at Brockport. "What did you do that for?" Deacon asked him.

"Ain't gonna run no more," he said. "I done it. Just like you said I could. Don't have to run no more."

He never did. Not one stride. It was enough that now people knew he could. And when they drop by the garage where Jackie works, he knows they remember the boy who could outrun the wind.

Example: Michael was 12 years old when diagnosed with an inoperable brain tumor. He joined The Winners Club. One day when they were alone, Deacon asked him, "Michael, have you ever had a dream for yourself?"

Michael told him he had always wanted to see the ocean, and again Deacon made a promise. Not long after that, after the doctor sadly shook his head,
250

Michael's mother called Deacon and said, "If you are really going to take Michael to see the ocean, you have to go now."

He is a man whose bank account for 25 years was limited to his for-pay job in the juvenile justice system. Not one dime from The Winners Club has ever found its way to his pocket. But within hours he had arranged for an airplane, a deep-sea charter and a hotel.

His eyes glistened as he retold the story on his front porch on Sugar Valley Road. "Oh, that Michael, he taught me more than I've ever taught anybody. He taught me how to die" As they sat beside the ocean, listening to its primordial cadence, the 12-year-old boy said he was more afraid for those he would leave behind than for himself. "I am special. I'll be all right."

Deacon began to sway slowly in the white porch swing. "We had secrets, him and me. We'd wink and that was the sign not to tell. But someday I'd like to write all that Michael told me. I visit his grave and I wink, and I seem to hear him say, 'You gonna tell, ain't you? You never could keep a secret.'"

Near the front of The Winners Club is a statue of

Inez holding a child in her arms.

She has been with Michael for six years now. Deacon lives next door. Alan Robinson supervises The Winners Club. Deacon no longer works as a juvenile justice counselor. He quit after he saw a photo of a boy shot through the head. Eventually, the children dropped off at the club were different from the Jackies and the Michaels and the Charlies. Long ago, little children could become such inspirations they would lift their parents with their miraculous dedication and spirit. Now 13-year-olds who make their own methamphetamines are placed on the doorsteps, their family structure disintegrated by dysfunctional parents beyond restructure, who would give the kids away if they could.

"I discovered that I could help innocent children, but I did not know how to help today's parents," he said. "And so I burned out and retired December 31, 2003."

Or so he thought.

One day long ago a man asked him to take some special children camping. Not long ago, missionaries Michael and Brenda Cooper told him he was needed in Haiti. There were children there. Innocent children

252

who were born hungry and would probably die hungry.

By puddle-jumper plane that landed in a long field, by pickup truck with eight other passengers, by walking, Deacon came to the village of Roi. The settlement has no electricity, no running water, no doctor. He saw bone-thin children in a desolate preschool and several of them would be dead in months from malnutrition, worms or parasites. In Roi he saw Down's syndrome, he saw faces distorted by cleft palates, he saw children who did not dream because they lived not by hope, but by an unexplainable instinct for survival, each day like all the others. And he saw innocence. Everywhere he looked he saw innocence and he understood he had not volunteered; he had been chosen by something higher to help children who are innocent.

"If somebody will back me, I will try to change their world one precious child at a time," he said. He will teach them to read so they can find in the Bible that they do have hope and a future. He will teach the physically challenged a skill knowing in their society even with an education and a skill they will always be known as a beggar. He will try to feed them more than the one bowl of rice and beans a day. Even in the hell

253

of Haiti, he just knows he can make them winners.
One by one.

Memorial to our Angel, Inez "Mama" Balliew

Memorial to an Angel

Just out of Calhoun on the Sugar Valley Road sits a very impressive 20-foot semicircular red brick memorial. Standing inside is a statue of a beautiful lady holding a baby in her arms; on its pedestal is inscribed "Suffer the Little Children."

The children this lady loved and cared for say, if one will observe closely, they can feel this ladies' love. Everyone who knew the lady has no doubt when looking at her likeness that she is about to speak.

All that knew and loved her believe that God has chosen this very special Christian lady as one of His angels, because of such love and affection she had for children.

Angels, according to many religions, are spiritual beings created by God. According to religious traditions, angels live in heaven and act as God's servants and as messengers between God and human beings. They also serve as guardians of individuals.

And those who knew her believe she still has knowledge of her loved ones, sitting beside God always being His servant, and helping Him to guard and take care of the children.

To those unfamiliar with this lady, it would perhaps appear to be the statue of a very prosperous, famous lady—a highly successful one at the least.

Who would guess that this is a memorial that a caring community dedicated to a lady, who dreamed of children succeeding, dreams that would eventually come true?

These dreams were planted like seeds in the hearts and minds of Inez Balliew and her family. They were dreams of the mentally handicapped, emotionally disturbed and physically handicapped children doing things no one else ever believed they could do. They were dreams that, once sprouted, grew in the hearts and minds of the Balliews and their children.

And the dreams are not yet over; they will never be over because of the beliefs she and her family were able to instill in the lives of their troubled children. Believing and teaching their children that they had control of their own minds and could with love and absolute desire see their own dreams come true.

Those beliefs are changing lives every day now because of Inez Balliew.

The angel lady's belief, which today has become

a trademark of the Balliews, "With God's help and work we can break the molds out of which these children were formed."

Inez Balliew always believed and loved her children with that very thought always in mind, a belief that still lives on in the minds of her children and their children.

She stated many times, "God made all of us, and God does not make mistakes. We adults are the ones who make them [mistakes]. We must never forget that every child was created perfect, because we know he was created in God's image."

More than 600 children over the years, with all sorts of problems, suddenly found a true friend, one who continually showed them absolute love.

When the children felt her love and encouragement they seemed to always want to succeed. They suddenly found that a pathway leading to self-confidence and self-esteem had opened up, and on that path Mrs. Inez Balliew and family always walked with them.

She had a gift that very few people could ever hope to have. She could make children feel loved the first time they saw her.

In the past 37 years, she saw, and several people believe she still sees, many things happen that could perhaps be considered miracles that her love created.

She once encouraged a shy little mentally-challenged girl who liked to sing, and was repaid when we watched the girl sing Amazing Grace for the president of the United States, Jimmy Carter.

Inez and Mrs. Rosalyn Carter

She shed tears of joy when one of the girls graduated from college and became a teacher of small children. She saw a girl that was headed straight for

258

serious trouble that is today a college graduate and a very successful businesswoman.

She saw a young man who was considered for a special class for the mentally limited receive a football scholarship to a major college and make the dean's list, and was elated when that young man received his master's degree.

A very small, mentally-challenged 8-year-old boy who could not talk… still in a diaper without any knowledge of personal hygiene… who knew nothing about clothing himself… who had to be tied in a chair in kindergarten to keep from hurting himself or others… came to live with her after she had raised two sons of her own. She was thrilled when this same young man received a special education diploma and received in his senior year, an award for 13 years of perfect school attendance.

She watched with pride as several of the ones she tutored became the first of their families to graduate from high school and watched eight of them graduate from college.

And when any of her former children came back to visit, bringing their own children, she would always say, "I love them like they are our grandchildren."

259

These "grandchildren" are far different children than their parents were, because their parents have them in church and parent them with compassion, true unselfish caring and love, That combination can always, with God's love and help, produce successful children.

Starting with her two sons the name "Mama" was the name she has been lovingly called by the hundreds of children she loved and helped raise.

How she was able to create the desire to succeed in so many young children was astounding, and lots of people thought, and now firmly believe, it was miraculous.

To watch her in action was like watching love in its truest form. You would witness such tenderness as she worked with the children, scolding them for not doing their very best, yet in her scolding she would be bolstering their pride because it was done with such love and gentleness.

Someone once said you can't fool a child about love; they recognize the real thing and respond accordingly. Every time the children returned home from a visit with Mrs. Balliew they were determined to do better, because it was expected, and they loved her and did not want to disappoint her.

Inez Balliew did so many things with her kids, it is difficult to list them all. She loved to sing with the children and, so her voice accompanies theirs on six recordings. She and the girls grew gardens, canned vegetables, won many blue ribbons for their efforts at the county fair, learned how to manage honeybees, took field trips, raised plants in their greenhouse, cooked and baked, planted flower gardens.

Inez Balliew's Award-winning Cub Scout Pack #139

Mrs. Balliew taught the girls how to sew and had many sessions concerning girls' ethics, values and morals. She and the children attended church together, and she always encouraged each of the children and their parents to attend church as a family—and many times was successful.

For several summers, handicapped children from Northern Ireland visited the Balliews for six weeks under the auspices of the Children's Friendship Project for Northern Ireland, an opportunity customarily reserved for "normal kids."

Inez Balliew requested handicapped girls be sent and in turn, was invited to visit Northern Ireland by the Lord Mayor of Belfast and school officials to show their gratitude for her volunteering to share many of her summers with their Catholic and Protestant handicapped children in the mountains of North Georgia.

Inez Balliew always tried to teach all her children that there are no limitations in life, only missed opportunities. Her job was simply to help cut down on the number of opportunities that her kids usually missed.

She was very difficult to thank or praise, because she simply did what she loved to do—to be with her children she loved so much and expect them to be successful. And to Inez Balliew that was nothing special.

All of these achievements were accomplished by a caring community that supported her in her attempts to help troubled children.

Inez said, "The Lord gave us the opportunity to see many of His miracles happen. There was no other way to explain how these people accomplished so many seemingly impossible things."

When God decided he needed Mrs. Inez "Mama" Balliew in heaven several of her girls agreed that he needed an angel to sit by Him, be His attendant and help Him with His children's miracles.

Today there are visitors from different parts of the country who come to see for themselves the lady with the angel look that was formed by a master sculptor in Rome, Italy. He used marble from the same quarries that have supplied the stone for centuries used to build magnificent buildings, memorializing God's saints and Roman noblemen.

The visitors carry away with them a feeling of love and better understanding of a saint when they remember the messages they see and read etched in a tablet of marble inside the memorial.

It is a message her family and the hundreds of children she loved wanted all to remember and many

263

were responsible for helping Mr. Balliew write. It goes thus:

I often thought as night draws nigh,
Of the Winners Club on the hill
With its yard so wide and blossom filled
Where the children played at will.
And when the night at last came down
Hushing the merry din,
Mama would always look around and ask
"Daddy, are all the children in?"
Oh, it's only been a short time since then,
And the clubhouse on the hill
Still echoes to children's feet
And the yard is never still.
But I see it as shadows creep,
And though it's only be a while since then,
I can still hear Mama ask,
"Daddy are all the children in?"
I wonder if when the shadows fall
On my last short earthly day,
When I prepare to say goodbye to the world outside
And I'm tired of earthly play
And when I finally reach the promised land
Where Mama so long has been,
I know I will hear Mama asking as of old,
"Are all the children in?"

Be this lady an angel or a saint, the babies she held when they were scared, abused, when they were sick, when they were about to be removed from their parents because of their being neglected, or had parents in conflict and had been taken to jail. To those hundreds of babies she held it didn't matter; she was both saint and angel. All they cared to know was, someone loved them and it stopped their crying and they fell asleep in her arms. The baby our angel holds in her arms represents her love for little children.

Mrs. Inez "Mama" Balliew deserves an important place in our community's history. There are many successful families in our community today because of her love and her God-given knowledge of how to bring an end to many generations of neglect.

God loved Inez "Mama" Balliew enough to teach her how to break molds.

Our guardian angel firmly believed and taught all her children and their families that they were to take care of their own families' needs and if they did they would not have time to judge others and their family's actions or deeds; only God is to judge others and their deeds.

She stated many times, "Ask God for the answer

to your troubles and He will help you take care of them."

How many people or children know for sure they have a guardian angel sent by God to protect them and who it is? Many of the lives Inez Balliew touched know personally and love their guardian angel. And it's been thought that God has designated Inez "Mama" Balliew as our own troubled children's guardian angel.

Inez Balliew went to heaven, fulfilling her duty as God's angel on Jan. 10, 1999 and since that day, hundreds of people have stopped and looked at the memorial to an angel, established by a community that loved and cherished her.

Attributions

"Deacon Balliew and His Winner's Club" – written by Roy Exum for *The Chattanooga News-Free Press*, 1986, and subsequently also published in a condensed version in *Readers' Digest* in 1986

"The House of Dreams" – written by Barry Giornelli for *The Calhoun Times*,

"Deacon of Hope" – written by Lee Walburn for *Atlanta Magazine*, August 2005

"The Winners Club" written by Tony Reynolds, and extracted from his book, TAPE IT TO YOUR HEART (published by Christian Services Network, ISBN-13 978-1593522513)

Printed in the United States
105595LV00001B/1-99/P

9 781603 640039